A Historical and Theoretical Guide to Studying Religion

Wesley A. Kort

ANTHEM PRESS

Anthem Press
An imprint of Wimbledon Publishing Company
www.anthempress.com

This edition first published in UK and USA 2024
by ANTHEM PRESS
75–76 Blackfriars Road, London SE1 8HA, UK
or PO Box 9779, London SW19 7ZG, UK
and
244 Madison Ave #116, New York, NY 10016, USA

© Wesley A. Kort 2024

The author asserts the moral right to be identified as the author of this work.

All rights reserved. Without limiting the rights under copyright reserved above, no part of this publication may be reproduced, stored or introduced into a retrieval system, or transmitted, in any form or by any means (electronic, mechanical, photocopying, recording or otherwise), without the prior written permission of both the copyright owner and the above publisher of this book.

British Library Cataloguing-in-Publication Data
A catalogue record for this book is available from the British Library.

Library of Congress Cataloging-in-Publication Data
A catalog record for this book has been requested.
2023946084

ISBN-13: 978-1-83999-054-0 (Hbk)
ISBN-10: 1-83999-054-6 (Hbk)

Cover Credit: Art by Edgar Boevé, (1929–2019)

This title is also available as an e-book.

CONTENTS

Preface		v
Introduction		ix
Part One: Historical		
1.	Modernity, Romanticism, and the Rise of Religious Studies	3
2.	Studying Religion and Cultural Faults Caused by Repression and Neglect	15
3.	Studying Religion and the Lack of Cultural Accesses to Needed Intangibles	35
4.	Studying Religion and the Cultural Need for More Adequate Worldviews	57
Part Two: Theoretical		
5.	The Object of Religious Studies	79
6.	The Position of the Person Studying Religion	99
7.	Taking into Account Religion's Excesses and Complexities	117
8.	Studying Religion while Being Religious	129
Conclusion		143
Index		157

PREFACE

The primary purpose of this book is to provide readers who are unfamiliar with the academic study of religion with a guide to what is now often called "religious studies." Such readers would, of course, include students, but I also have in mind potential readers who are interested in the study of religion but are unfamiliar with the field because they are not located in contexts where "religious studies" developed and is widely established. The field has its primary location in the United States, but it has moved beyond those borders to include anglophone and other contexts. Within and beyond those contexts are potential readers who study religion but are unfamiliar with "religious studies" as an academic field.

A less obvious purpose of this book is to address what I consider to be an important problem in and for religious studies that needs more attention brought to it and more guidance toward its amelioration. That problem is the difference and even tension between a study of religion that is religiously based or directed and a study of religion that is not, that is nonreligious or secular. While this book does not address this problem fully and, even more, does not solve it, the problem is a recurring topic in it. The lack of a solution is due to the problem's complexity, but it should, nevertheless, be dealt with because it carries the potential for weakening and even threatening the role of religious studies in academic culture.

This problem threatens the field because these two approaches to the study of religion are contrary to one another. In addition, present in academic culture are interests that are directed not toward resolving or even reducing the problem but of acting upon it. This can occur, for example, by locating the study of religion in one or the other of two locations, either in religiously designated locations, such as in chaplaincies or nearby faculties of religion and theology, or in departments that are secular, especially departments in the social sciences. This separation has been aggravated by developments on both sides. On the secular side, it can be said that the social sciences, while they are traditionally located between the natural sciences and the humanities, have become increasingly oriented to the natural sciences, taking a more naturalist or materialist approach to their field, including religion. On the other, religious, side, it can be said that religious and theological approaches to the study of religion have become, for reasons at which we shall look later in this book, more centripetal than centrifugal, more internally than externally oriented.

The problem as it now presents itself is too substantial and complex to be altered by a single attempt. But it is hoped that the actual and apparently growing separation of the two approaches from one another can be eased by clarifying the basis upon which an increased rapprochement between them can be achieved.

This problem and responses to it have been integral to my work in religious studies from the beginning, more than half a century ago. It began in the college and theological seminary that I attended with the goal of entering Christian ministry in the Dutch Calvinist denomination in which my father had served as a pastor until his death when I was eight years old. I found the religious and theological bases and orientations of these institutions to be confining. This was despite the fact that they were influenced in great part by what was referred to as a "world and life" view, which was based on John Calvin himself and, more specifically, on the work and views of Abraham Kuyper, the Dutch Reformed intellectual who advocated the worthiness of religious involvement with the various aspects of the wider political and cultural world. Having majored as an undergraduate in English literature and retaining my interest in religion despite disappointment with my denomination, I applied for admission to the graduate program in Religion and Literature at the University of Chicago with the intention not so much to gain a graduate degree as to deepen and broaden my knowledge of religion and its relation to culture and literature.

When I began my graduate work at Chicago, I soon recognized that the study of religion was carried on less out of a religious base and with religious goals but in more objective, especially social scientific, and philosophical ways. While being sustained by my growing involvement in literary and cultural studies, I continued to work toward relating them to religious topics and interests. This was aided by the addition to the faculty of scholars more clearly related to Christian interests, especially Lutheran. While I managed to clarify some bases for securing relations between literary or cultural studies and religion, such as the importance of both textuality and narrative discourse, I continued also to be aware of the dynamics of contrariness in academic and the broader culture between religion and Western modernity. I emerged from my graduate work with some strategies for handling the problem but not with ways of resolving it.

When in 1963 I accepted my first faculty appointment, a temporary position in the Department of Religion at Princeton University, I encountered the problem again. I soon recognized that of the dozen or so members of the faculty in religion, almost half of them were identifiable as Christian theologians of one kind or another. This recognition was supported by the identity of others on the faculty, primarily its younger members, who were identifiable not religiously but by their methods, especially sociological and philosophical. The differences were apparent but, I hasten to say, not damaging. There was mutual understanding and respect, but, engaged as I was with the problem and its importance, I was aware of it and could speak to representatives on both sides about it.

After two years on the faculty at Princeton, I accepted an appointment to the Department of Religion at Duke University, where I was fortunate to remain for forty-nine years. When I arrived, I was surprised by and interested in many aspects of life there, particularly its location in the South and its continuity with that location. For example, the first black student to do so graduated from Duke in the spring of my first year. Equal to my interest in matters of that kind was the practice of opening departmental meetings with Protestant prayer. This was modified when a few years later Jewish scholars were added to the department, having results for the content but not the practice of praying, until a few years later when it was abandoned. I soon recognized that this and the identities of the faculty were traceable to the department's indebtedness for its existence to the Divinity School.

The constitution of the department's faculty was gradually affected by the hiring of scholars able to offer courses in traditions other than those pervasive in Western culture, a need that grew rapidly in response to student interest. Scholars in Islamic studies, Buddhism, and Hinduism were added. This did not radically affect the problem created by differing attitudes regarding the relation for studying religion of religious to nonreligious bases and aims. This was because these new faculty were themselves identifiable with the religious traditions that they represented. Religious interests were more diversified but not obviously lessened.

At the same time, there were, during the closing decades of the twentieth century, changes in academic culture toward more criticism and suspicion not only among faculty in the social sciences but also in the humanities concerning the relation of cultural investments and values to political and social interests, especially to power and its uses to elevate and sustain some portions of the society at the expense of others. This critical method was attributable, although not exclusively, to Marx and Freud and to a more materialist and less idealist account of culture. The evaluation of religion along these lines was included. This change of stance or method affected the relation of departmental members to one another and of the department as a whole to its neighbors on both sides. There was a noticeable shift of direction toward closer ties with other academic departments, especially the social sciences, than with the Divinity School. As we shall see later in this book, there were several reasons for this shift of orientation or interest in academic culture generally and in the study of religion particularly. While gradual and complex, these changes were among those that created a departmental ethos that, when I retired in 2014, was sharply different from the department I entered in 1965.

This enduring problem, namely, the difference, distance, and even tension between two approaches to the study of religion, is pervasive in this guide. I am grateful for the exposure to the problem that was provided by the various academic positions I held. I take my own experiences, however limited, to support the assumption that in many other places, at least in the United States and perhaps more widely, this problem is detectable and consequential. To repeat, I do not claim to have resolved it. But I do hope that it can be eased and its damaging possibilities averted.

What is needed is agreement on both sides that the other side has value and deserves inclusion, in varying proportions, of what can bring the two approaches more closely into accord. On the nonreligious or secular side, there cannot be an assumption that religion is basically attributable to something else, something, in a word, less worthy, such as the gaining and validating of a power that elevates some people at the expense of others. Religion should not be reduced to something less than it is, although it is always related to such things. And, on the other side, there cannot be an attempt to discount religion's relation and even indebtedness to human culture, no turning of religion toward a basis for exclusion and superiority. The easing depends on regard by each side for the interests of the other. More important, perhaps, is a higher regard, than seems commonly present, for positions that establish their identity less by their contrary relations to their alternatives and more by their relations to them. Positions that are not primarily secured by opposition to their contraries but by drawing from them are more difficult to formulate and sustain. It is somewhere in this middle position that increased rapprochement can be anticipated and, I think, found. At least attainable is the exchange of the problem from its being a threat to the study of religion to its being a challenge and an opportunity for its enrichment and increased relevance.

INTRODUCTION

The academic study of religion or, as it is now often called, "religious studies, is a scholarly field that evolved primarily in the United States. While its complexity contributes to its richness and challenges, it also at times seems to suggest or anticipate incoherence and, worse, tension and conflict. These conditions and the possible threats they carry have given rise to this book, which is an attempt first of all to account for the complexity and diversity of the field and then to suggest ways by which some major differences and contrary interests can be brought into closer relations with one another. It is hoped that matters accounting for differences and even tensions in the field are revealed to be less determining than matters encompassing those differences or relating them more closely to one another. It should be said at the outset that woven throughout this account is the opinion that a major difficulty in the field is the difference within it of religious and nonreligious approaches to the study of religion. This difference defies full resolution, but it need not divide the field. Indeed, the differences and tensions created by it can be shown, it is hoped, to contribute to the field's richness.

I

It is important, first of all, to see religious studies as we now know it, as having its origins approximately two centuries ago. Those origins were sponsored by scholars who, for the most part, can be identified as social scientists. This means that the academic study of religion had its origins less in the religious identities or interests of scholars than in an academic interest in religion as a recurring component of human life and cultures, often cultures of the distant past or of distant parts of the globe. However, while we now think of the social sciences as more related to the natural sciences than to the humanities, as more marked by objectivity and description than by concern for human well-being, the social sciences as they developed carried within them humanistic ties to, among other things, moral philosophy and philosophical anthropology. That is, the social sciences carried with them interests in the moral and spiritual well-being of persons and cultures, and those concerns, as we shall see, were an ingredient in the attention given by many of them to religion.

The humanistic or ethical concerns of the social sciences in religion can be seen as having taken two directions. One was the recognition of religion as a matter relating Western modernity to other and often distant cultures. Religion could be seen as a shared, enduring, and embedded part of human life and cultures rather than as occasional or superficial. Second, these scholars were aware not only that their own culture was marked by an increasing separation of human concerns from religious understandings of and directives for them but also that the retraction of religious concerns in modernity exposed lacunae and needs in the culture that carried consequences potentially contrary to human well-being. These two directions were combined so that the study of religion in early or distant cultures revealed, among many other things, that the deficiencies of modern Western culture did not appear in these other contexts because they were avoided or filled by religious beliefs and practices. Religious studies, then, did not arise only from an objective, disinterested, or scientific curiosity about human life and cultures but also from concern about the relation of religion to sustaining or increasing human well-being.

This does not mean that scholars engaged in this work all agreed about the relevance of religion to modern Western culture. For some religion, although perhaps in modified forms, could be viewed as still active in and relevant to present conditions, still having actual or potential relations to human needs and difficulties that were helpful or beneficial. Others, however, concluded that, while religion addressed the human needs and potentials of people in the past and of some people living in the present, religion did not and could not have a significant place and role in modern culture. For them, to be modern meant the diminishing role of religion and an increasing role of science and technology. However, despite important differences such as this, a generally shared conclusion was that religion played and continues for many to play important roles in human cultures because it is, among other things, a response to needs and potentials integral to human life and well-being. These human needs and potentials continue, and, if they are not addressed religiously, they call for and even require the attention of some other, that is nonreligious, kind.

During the nineteenth and twentieth centuries, skepticism concerning religion's continuing role in Western modernity increased while at the same time the prestige of the natural sciences and technology increased. These dynamics drew the social sciences increasingly away from their humanistic and ethical attachments and more toward scientific, secular, and materialistic methods and interests. This process was abetted by a strand of religious critique that took religion to be not simply outmoded but actually harmful relative to human needs and potentials. By the mid-twentieth century, the secularization of higher education, except in religiously identifiable institutions, had diminished the academic study of religion from its place as integral and shared to more peripheral and scattered locations.

II

However, in the middle decades of the twentieth century, the place and role of the study of religion in higher education changed. It became more visible and specific, regaining some of the ground or standing it had lost. The study of religion not only became less dependent on the interests and methods of other disciplines but also was motivated as much by religious as by academic interests. The outward sign of this change was the rapid creation or expansion of departments or programs for the study of religion in institutions with no religious identities or with ties to religion that had faded or been severed.

A very important feature of this change in the academic study of religion was that it not only was freed from dependence on other disciplines but also that it served to increase the role of religious reasons for the study of religion. Studying religion came to be related more than it had been to being religious. This change of mind concerning the study of religion from an increasingly secular academic understanding of it to a more noticeably religious interest in it gave rise to larger numbers and sizes of departments of religion, especially in institutions that were not themselves religiously identifiable. It is not too much to say that in the second half of the twentieth century, most academic institutions in the United States established or expanded departments or programs for the study of religion.

Reasons for the change not only in the visibility and role of the academic study of religion but also in the religious interest in religion can be given. One is that the increasingly secular character of much higher education during the first half of the twentieth century diminished the assumption that academic culture and other departments or disciplines could be counted on to carry forward on their own the moral and spiritual norms and values that had traditionally been part of higher education. This fading of attention to religious values and norms in academic culture seems to have warranted intervention and change.

A second and equally important reason for the change was the greater awareness of religion resulting from the experiences of the Second World War, not only the enormous loss of human life but also a cultural uncertainty about the future created by the development and deployment of atomic weapons. In addition, the war raised awareness that the conflicts threatening world stability had religious and not only political, social, or economic bases. Religion could be seen to have played in other countries a basic and causal role in human lives, relationships, and cultures rather than a secondary, occasional, or derivative one. An academic waning of interest in religion and the assumption that religion is something superficial or idiosyncratic in human cultures could be seen as naïve or misguided.

A third reason was the rising threat of communism, which was interpreted in the West less as an economic or political formation than as a non- and even anti-religious ideological force threatening to spread over large parts of the world. Being religious and resisting this threat moved toward a more central place in Western political and national interests and identities. In the United States, the religious ingredient in the cold war can be seen specifically and publicly in congressional decisions of the 1950s to print "In God We Trust" on currency and to add "under God" to the pledge of allegiance to the flag. The cold war was also a war about religion.

A fourth reason, one to which attention was drawn by the sociologist of religion Will Herberg, lies with descendants of the large numbers of people who emigrated to the United States at the end of the nineteenth and beginning of the twentieth centuries, numbers that affected the national population both by number and diversity. By mid-century, the grandchildren of these immigrants were willing to exchange their ethnic identities for religious ones, such as being not so much a Polish American as an American Catholic. This desire of the third generation to remember what the second generation tended to forget included religion, even if only personal versions of it.

A fifth reason was that, as Herberg also pointed out, while, unlike many Western nations, there was no state religion, being American also came to mean being a religious person of some kind or at least having respect for religion. Having a religious identity, however faint or improvised, provided a way of being an American of a particular kind and of being particular in a generally recognizable and acceptable way.

Finally, the global extent of the war and the consequent increase of the West's awareness of and relations to other, particularly Asian, cultures supported attention to the place and role of religion in them. These religions themselves came increasingly to be of interest to Western students not only because of the inherent qualities of those religions but also because of their perceived relevance to a generation of students looking for alternative and more personal, spiritual, and non-conforming ways of being religious. Students enrolled in classes dealing with world, especially Asian, religions, and they did so in large measure for religious reasons.

While the rise, during the second half of the twentieth century, of religious interests in academic culture and the institutional recognition of religious studies as justifying increased independence and visibility, the founding and expanding of departments or programs for the study of religion did not wait for a plan that would guide their formations, especially their relations to other departments in Arts and Sciences in which the study of religion, although occasional, was still being carried on. Institutions that had lingering religious ties faced less uncertainty about how religious studies should be formed; they could return to those earlier resources or interests. But matters were more unsettled in public institutions and in institutions that, while they may have had religious ties in their founding, had become more identified with secular academic interests than with the religious identities of their pasts.

Rather than drawing up and sharing a plan for founding, expanding, or reconstituting departments for the study of religion, institutions that were undetermined by religious identities faced the question of what the curriculum of such a department should consist and, even more basically, from where faculty for it should be sought. The answer to the second of these questions was counted on to answer the first, leaving those hired to formulate a rationale for the department and to clarify its curricular structure and aims. A determining factor in this development was that institutions with faculties offering doctoral programs in the study of religion and producing graduates who could be hired were most often institutions with religious, particularly Protestant, identities, often schools of divinity or theological seminaries. This meant that the pool of scholars for filling faculty positions in new or expanding departments consisted largely of people trained in the traditional subjects of the Protestant theological curriculum, biblical studies, the history of Western Christianity, and Christian theology and ethics. Catholic and Jewish studies could, sooner or later, be accommodated by this Protestant core because both shared an interest in biblical studies and both had histories relevant to the history of Protestant Christianity.

Faculty for the new or expanded departments, then, because many, if not most, of them were trained in Protestant institutions, were more accustomed to relate to theologically or religiously identifiable colleagues in their own or other institutions than to either the faculty of the Arts and Sciences division of which they were now also a part or to the history of religious studies that was mentioned earlier and that we shall trace in the first part of this book. These conditions meant that newly hired faculty, drawn as they were largely from Protestant institutions and graduate programs, would shape the curricula of new departments according to their own religious identities and training.

These conditions—the rapid pace of founding and expanding departments, the lack of shared blueprints for their position and role in the Arts and Sciences, and the prominence of the Protestant theological curriculum for newly hired faculty—created tensions when it became clearer that departments, by their place in Arts and Sciences, should also be related to other departments, should include more than the study of Christianity or Western religions, and should be aware of or even consistent with the kinds of scholarship to which we shall, in the first part of this book, turn. These complications were intensified in the opening decades of the second half of the century by the sharply increased interest, both within the wider culture and among students, in Asian religions, especially Hinduism and Buddhism.

III

It is not too much to say that during the second half of the twentieth century, the roles and effects of the nonreligiously based religious studies that we shall look at in the first part of this book came gradually to dilute or replace the bases on which the post-war increase in the visibility of and reasons for studying religion had been built. Scholars such as those at whose work we shall look in the first part of this book became more influential, and religious studies came to be less religiously identified and more like the study of religion in other Arts and Sciences departments.

However, it is important to recognize and remember that there were two differing sources that gave rise to religious studies as we now know it. One source, the more recent one, was the founding and expanding of departments of religious studies after the Second World War when there was a noticeable increase of interest in religious reasons for studying religion. The other source was the kind of religious studies that we shall trace in the first part of this book. Religious studies as we now know it has, therefore, two sources and influences that sufficiently differ from one another to raise uncertainties and even tensions concerning their relations to one another and to their differing institutional ties, on the one side to other departments where religion is studied and, on the other side, to other forms of religiously framed academic interests in religion, chaplains on campus or theological faculties in other institutions. It created a noticeable distinction between religious studies sponsored by interests identifiable as religious and religious studies sponsored nonreligiously and determined by various academic disciplines. The convergence of these two orientations was met less by attempts to relate them to one another or to resolve the differences between them than by living with the differences and even tensions between them.

This difference or divide, however, while important and continuing, was eased by several factors. One of them was the interest of both sides in historical studies and methods. Historical studies were part of a religiously based study of religion because of the importance of a religion's origins and developments for understanding it, something especially important for scholars influenced by Protestant emphases on understanding Christianity first of all by beginning with biblical texts. Historical studies and methods had also been important for the rise of religious studies in the nineteenth century, especially an interest in early cultures, their histories, and the importance of religion for understanding them. For these reasons, history and historical studies came to prominence for the study of religion and offered a basis for shared interests within departments of religious studies and between them and other faculties in the Arts and Sciences.

This degree of compatibility between religiously and nonreligiously based forms of studying religion, while not complete, gave to departments of religious studies support for accommodating methods and interests housed primarily in departments of the social sciences. An enlarged pool of prospective candidates for faculty appointments in religious studies came into view, candidates trained in other Arts and Sciences disciplines. This helped to relate religious studies to other academic faculties. Indeed, it is not too much to say that faculty members in departments of religious studies became, by the end of the twentieth century, related as often to members of other Arts and Sciences faculties as to other faculty in their own departments. This development served to produce noticeable differences between the two kinds of approaches and scholarly relations. The department's faculty members were not as able to assume as they once did a unified understanding of the bases and goals of the department. They came less to be communities with a shared understanding and rationale of the department and more groups of individuated scholars related as much or even more to colleagues outside their department than to those within it.

A second factor affecting the constitution of departments of religious studies is that each of the two sources or traditions for the study of religion, namely, secular and religious, changed. In a word, each side became more closely identified with the methods and goals of their own training and orientation than with one another. The sense of a shared basis between the two sides was weakened. The study of religion that was religiously based became more noticeably religious, and the nonreligiously based study of religion became more noticeably secular.

The social sciences shifted in orientation more toward the natural sciences, more influenced by their methods and goals, and less marked by humanistic and ethical concerns. Most importantly, the assumption that research should have two characteristics became prominent, namely, the tracing of what is studied to its causal base and the understanding of this base in materialist terms, that is, in terms of matter and energy or power. This shift in the social sciences was dependent, although certainly not solely, on the influence of Karl Marx and Sigmund Freud. The shift was also supported by the increasingly shared assumption in academic culture that what can profitably be talked about and what provides common ground and potential for scholarly and academic agreement in the social sciences and even in the humanities has this standing because what is under investigation or discussion can be to a major extent causally attributed or traced to materiality, that is, to matter and energy or power. When this assumption affects scholars in religious studies, religion tends to be treated as something other or less than what it presents itself or is generally taken to be. It becomes possible even to say that religion could or even should be understood primarily in relation to material, especially political, social, or economic, interests. Materialist assumptions created the possibility to study religion not as having a content, role, or standing of its own in human lives and cultures but as arising from and dependent on something nonreligious behind or below it. Aggravating the situation just described is the fact that materialist assumptions in academic culture carried with them the implication that religion should be viewed as something needing critically to be traced to what it conceals, namely, its nonreligious or materialist causes or uses, in many cases to human beings understood under the heading of *homo economicus*.

Corresponding or contrary changes occurred for those with religious interests in the study of religion. For reasons we shall look at more fully later in this book, a shift that affected religious studies was one that allowed for understandings of religious identity, traditions, and institutions that were more centripetal than centrifugal, more internally than externally oriented. This change, while having precedents in earlier stages of modernity, became increasingly noticeable and influential, particularly for Christian scholars. There had been, especially since the First World War, a rising critique of Western modernity not as a culture identified with the maturation and well-being of humanity but as driven by interests based on increasing the power of some to dominate others, often in order to exploit them. This critique of Western culture weakened the assumption that religious beliefs, practices, and institutions were obliged to understand or defend their identities to audiences outside their own institutional and discursive traditions and boundaries. Religion was increasingly seen in relation to itself and not to the larger, including academic, culture.

In a word, both religious and nonreligious interests in and for the study of religion came, toward the end of the twentieth century, more particularized.

This tendency or movement was supported by a waning of confidence in identifying as determining for human lives and cultures universally shared characteristics. It became increasingly clear that what was taken to be universal was more identifiable as something particularly Western and modern. Not only that, these universals came also to be seen as discounting or demoting the roles and standings of some peoples and the elevation of others, particularly an implicit evaluation and distinction based on such factors as race and gender.

A factor easing the difference between the two sides was the increasing awareness of and interest in other cultures. The importance for religious studies of what was called "other," "non-Western," or "World" religions became more visible. Faculties of religious studies increasingly were affected by scholars working on the history and present conditions of religions other than Christianity and Judaism. This change was due in part, as we saw earlier, to student interest in Asian religions, but it was also due to growing interests in "globalization." There was an increased awareness of diversity and differences brought about by world commerce and trade, changes in immigration laws and patterns, and wider access to modes of transportation.

IV

In recent decades, departments of religious studies have been affected by a curricular increase in the study of differing religions and in the number of faculty equipped to work in them and to teach them. This change was supported by both sides. For nonreligious interests, this increased presence of non-Western studies deflected attention away from the prominence and even dominance of Western, especially Protestant Christian, influences. On the other hand, however, it also increased the presence of religious interests in religious studies because faculty brought into departments of religious studies who were trained in other traditions were often themselves identified with and participants in the religion they were brought in to study and teach. Knowledge of and interest in other religions were most likely to be found in scholars brought up or educated in cultures and institutions identified with the religion. This rise in the number of courses and faculty specializing in non-Western religions changed the ethos of departments from an increasingly secular approach to the study of religion and toward a revival of religious interests in and reasons for studying it. Departments came more noticeably to be constituted by faculty identifiable as related to, if not representative of, the religion they studied and taught.

There are advantages to structuring departments for the study of religion by means of particular religions related to the religious identities of faculty.

For one thing, it makes visible the variety of religious traditions and cultures that can raise in students' minds questions and inferences not only about the differences and similarities between religions but also, due to their inclusion under the heading of "religions," about what religion itself is. Second, while it enlarges the religious bases for studying religion, it also modifies it. Even if faculty members are identified with the tradition they study and teach, they are at least not religiously exclusive. Third, if three or four religions form the curriculum of a department, it follows that, budgets or student interests allowing, more could be added. Plurality can imply universality. Fourth, it makes a department and its faculty members more immediately identifiable. Various religions are taught and studied, and, when a member of the faculty identifies him- or herself, this can be done simply and directly: a person does not teach or study religion but, instead, Judaism, Islam, or Hinduism. Particular religions provide more specific terms than "religion." In other words, there is a common, although questionable, cultural and academic assumption that, unlike "religion," "Islam" and "Buddhism" refer to something unified, particular, and important enough to be studied.

But disadvantages in this arrangement also appear. The first is that what allows for treating Islam or Buddhism as a particular and recognizable object of study is granted by distance. Someone born and raised in Western culture would not so easily think of Christianity in the same way, that is, as single, unified, and able to be abstracted from modern Western culture and history. It is difficult to think of Christianity as something distinct, single, and definable. It is variously formed and is as much integral to Western culture as it is identifiable as separable from it. The same can be said of other religions. It is distance from them that allows non-Western religions to be thought of as particular and abstract things.

Another disadvantage of having a department with faculty distinguishable by the religion they study and teach is the question of whether justice will be done to the tradition. As we shall see, major religions are not only complex but also inherently diverse and conflicted. A religion taught by a representative will likely be presented from a particular perspective or position. A department of religious studies so formed would be similar to a Political Science department that hires faculty not apart from their political convictions and affiliations but because of them so that a diversity of political opinions can be represented. One could argue that difficulties such as these would be modified if faculty identified with specific religious traditions were not themselves representatives of the religions but nonreligiously interested in them. But most scholars who focus on one religion are themselves personally involved with it. This is especially true for non-Western religions. It may be relatively easy to find faculty nurtured in modern Western culture who are themselves nonreligious but know a great deal about Judaism or Christianity, let us say, but those trained in other traditions, like Hinduism or Islam, are less likely to have been equally affected by modern Western scholarly principles and methods.

Finally, religious studies departments formed increasingly as a collection of scholars who represent major religions are less unified than they appear to be. This creates the obvious need for increasing shared goals and methods. What is particularly needed is a guide that leads to a shared understanding of what religion is and how and why it should be studied. In other words, the principal concern of a department of religion needs to be *religion*, and the secondary or dependent concern should be the relation of a religion or of religious people to that principal concern.

All of this brings us to the present situation, namely, that religious studies as a field needs more of a unifying basis and is more destabilized by the kinds of differences and uncertainties suggested above than faculty within such departments seem to address. The point is that, lacking coherence or more of a shared base, they are vulnerable from both sides: the Scylla of submitting religious studies to particular religious interests and the Charybdis of secular, materialist, and at times even anti-religious assumptions and methods. They are vulnerable to being absorbed by one side, by the other, or by both.

Little guidance in and through all of this can be sought from the major professional organization, The American Academy of Religion. It is itself, with its ties to the Society of Biblical Literature, marked by these tensions, less unified than its institutional existence would suggest, and standing primarily as a tent-like arena for a wide variety of particular interests and convictions operating under its institutional expanse. It is not as though members of the AAR all have something in common. Separations are wide, and groups of members often have little in common with other groups. Departments, graduate programs, professional societies, and a range of scholarly journals, rather than address uncertainty, institutionalize the complexities and conceal the problems caused by them.

It is in and toward the situation thus described that this book is located and aimed. It is motivated by the thought that the complexities and uncertainties of present conditions call for attention. It may be questionable to offer readers a guide to the study of religion that emphasizes unanswered questions, differences, and, even, tensions within the field and its vulnerability to outside interests, but I think this is both necessary and beneficial because the present situation, while uncertain and possibly unsustainable, is also challenging and rich. It puts the reader from the outset in a position of facing the complexities and uncertainties regarding the nature and role of religion and how it should be addressed, understood, and evaluated. While falling short of providing a fully adequate blueprint, it offers a guide to greater coherence and a shared method that can at least form the basis for further discussion both in the classroom and in the faculty lounge.

It is hoped that this guide makes its goal and direction sufficiently clear to be followed. The first point is that there are two sources or origins of religious studies. One of them is nonreligious and identified most fully with social science interests and methods. This first source must also be seen to carry a tradition of moral interests and values that are related to or sourced by religion. While, perhaps, truer in the past than now, to be oriented to and by the social sciences need not, as we shall see, make a scholar in religious studies indifferent toward moral and spiritual human well-being. The second source is religious, but it is religious in a way related to cultural needs, potentials, and threats. The second point, which is implied by the first, is that nonreligious and religious interests in the study of religion have points of relation that can provide a more shared basis for their co-existence and interaction. Finally, what is studied in religious studies is religion, and this depends on a clearer, more complex, and more dynamic understanding of what religion is. Answering this theoretical need, which will be attempted in the second half of this book, is presented as a directive that affects and relates to one another the diverse interests and methods gathered under the heading of religious studies.

V

Having indicated some of the difficulties and even tensions in religious studies, it is also important to say that there are already good reasons for affirming the standing and role of religious studies in higher education. If questions arise concerning the viability, suitability, or necessity of religious studies, answers can be given.

One question that can be raised about the viability of a department of religious studies is whether or not it builds on a lineage of scholarship and research that can be identified as sufficiently sound to provide an at least partial agenda of shared interests that those working in the field can be counted on to recognize and to have opinions about. Indeed, what constitutes the distinctive position of a discipline is precisely this, namely, its role as continuing a legacy of scholarship that is not constitutive of some other department or field. The answer to this first and quite basic question is affirmative. People in religious studies are the beneficiaries not only of a rich legacy of field work, research, and theorizing that is diverse and substantial but also of interests in the study of religion that are motivated largely by the assumption or conviction that religion and religious studies are culturally relevant and even needed. Previous work in the study of religion forms a complex and firm basis from which to measure advance or to project further continuities and departures. In support of this assertion, I have isolated three interests that appear and reappear in religious studies from the early nineteenth century and into the present century and are described in the first half of this book. I have selected scholars in that history who, while in many ways different from one another, can be identifiable as engaged by one or another of these three interests. My choice of interests or topics as well as of scholars attentive to them is selective and surely could be altered or extended. But I think that people working in religious studies share a background provided to them by the kind of scholars gathered in the first part of the book and by the interests in religion they pursue. While other topics and scholars who engage them could be added or substituted, those presented are worthy of attention not only by their positions in the past but also by their relevance to preset conditions. While this group of scholars is for the most part identifiable with the social sciences, they share as well what now is in the social sciences of less importance, namely, relating religion to human needs and potentials. This makes them as, if not more, important for religious studies than they are to the currently increasing materialist methods of the social sciences. In the second part of this book, I shall suggest that those with religious reasons for studying religion will be able, perhaps in their own and differing ways, to relate to the three topics or interests addressed in the first part of the book. Generally, it is the case that those studying religion for religious reasons can draw on ample resources to illuminate ways by which religion is directed to or can be, at least in part, understood as relevant to human needs and potentials. More specifically, it will be proposed that one of the constitutive factors in a religious interest in the study of religion is its relation to human needs and potentials so that relating religion to cultural lacks and problems does not represent a dilution or reduction of religion but is part of its very nature.

The second question that could be asked in a process of examining the viability of a field is whether work done within it continues to be of value. Just because there have been topics of importance and scholars of stature addressing them in the past does not mean that their work should be carried on. The question, then, is whether currently there are cultural and personal needs and faults to which religious studies is relevant and justifiably related. The answer I give to this question is that religious studies arose at a time when lacks or faults in modern Western culture were in various ways increasingly detected and directly addressed. A major form of this critique and address was provided by the rise of what we now call religious studies, especially by virtue of the combination in the history of religious studies of critical or diagnostic and remedial and salutary tasks. These tasks can be seen as appropriate for both nonreligious and religious interests in studying religion. The question, then, is whether or not these lacks have been filled or these faults mended, obviating the need to continue religious studies. My answer is that they have not been filled or healed; indeed, they have grown in gravity, and additional lacks and needs can be added to the three to which I shall draw attention. So, religious studies is a field of scholarship that is even more relevant to contemporary, including academic, culture than to the culture in which earlier interests in studying religion arose and academic work was carried on. Indeed, the legacy confirms that a department of religious studies is not in the business only for describing religion but also for understanding its nature and indicating its relations to human needs and potentials.

The third question concerns what primarily is studied in religious studies. The question is whether there is something that, by virtue of its own characteristics, stands out as identifiable, that is, as religious or as religion. Can we move from vague or popular assumptions about religion or from definitions projected by scholars with particular interests in religion to a more shareable and workable understanding of what religions are, why they differ, and what they have in common? Can there be at least partial or conditional agreement on this difficult but basic question? One of the items on the agenda of any department of religious studies should be an ongoing attempt to reach a degree of agreement on this question. Concerning it, a few things should be said in advance. First, religion is too entwined, positively or negatively, with other aspects of human lives and cultures to be separated out as a discrete or separate entity. Consequently, it is wise not to favor using the term in its nominal form. Indeed, it is not so much the study of religions that is basic to and defining of a department of religious studies but religion, and the basis for studying it is provided by religious people. If there are things, practices, and beliefs that are religious, they are because people produce, have, or perform them, and those who do so are religious people. As a consequence, what primarily is studied in religious studies are religious people, and the noun "religion" is used in this book as a convenient term arising from what makes the people being studied religious. It also should be said that some of the problems or objections arising from definitions of religion or religious is that they are often too simple or inflexible. A way of defining religion must be found that is more complex and flexible, especially one that anticipates and accounts for differences as well as similarities between people both of differing and of the same religions. In the second part of the book, I attempt to provide such a definition. Again, it is not proposed as final but as useful, especially to account for differences, even conflicts, between and within religions as well as similarities.

The fourth question that can be raised concerns the relations between the recurring interests or topics traced in the first part of this book and the characteristics of studying religion for religious reasons. Are the recurring topics in the emergence of religious studies and the structure and dynamics of religion as I identify them compatible? I think that they are. However, I shall also want to say that the understandings of religion evident in the work treated in the first part of the book are partial in their emphasis on one and not all of the religion-making characteristics or constitutive elements. I shall also want to propose that this is why those with religiously based interests for the study of religion are often critical of or resistant to the treatments of religion in departments of religious studies. But I shall also want to point out that this criticism is likely motivated by partial rather than by adequate understandings of religion. I take the partiality of both sides as an almost inevitable consequence rather than a fault. I shall also point out that this partiality on both sides exposes an opportunity or space between nonreligious approaches to the study of religion and approaches that are based on religious identities and affiliations, a space that it is the goal of this book at least partially to clarify as not only distinguishing both sides from but also relating both sides to one another.

A fifth question is whether the methods employed by the field are contrary to the religious identities of those who study religion. In other words, is it necessary that courses in religious studies will make students less religious? This question is similar to a question of this kind posed by or to a field in which something of value is at stake, music, for example, or literature. There is no doubt that in the study of religion, evaluation comes into play. What justifies interest in the study of religious people and what is questionable, even off-putting, in a religion or its adherents are both of scholarly interest. This leads to the question of whether religion is or is not in itself a good thing. I know of faculty in religious studies whose answer to this question is negative. This is tolerable, but only to an extent. Can any department expect to continue if the aim of its investigations is to discredit, marginalize, or dissolve the object of its study or reduce it to something else? However, there is also no doubt that religious studies will make those engaged in it more critical, more aware of negatives and what causes them, than they otherwise would be. But that is also true for the study of literature. The elevated position of selected literary texts, the so-called canon, has recently been subverted, and departments of literature have upset priorities and traditional evaluative standards. But critical stances can result in new appreciations. There is no doubt that religious studies will make students more aware of negative and even objectionable aspects of religion than otherwise they would be, but it also should make them more aware than they otherwise would be of why the activities, beliefs, and artifacts of religious people deserve to be understood and taken seriously.

This question carries implications for the relations of religious studies to the religious identities of students engaged in it. There is nothing unusual about this question. It arises in political science when knowledge of political dynamics and goals has an effect on a student's own political persuasions. In addition, at least some students take courses in psychology because they have questions about their own psychological well-being. The same is true, mutatis mutandis, for religious studies. Students should be able to relate what is being studied to their own religious identities or lack of them. And this should not only be negative. True, students come into class with assumptions about religion that need to be questioned, but the primary pedagogical objective of a religious studies department should not be to undermine or discredit religion. A responsible critique should also be constructive. When religion is criticized, what it is for the sake of which the critique of it is launched should be made clear. Anti-religion is not an alternative position to being religious. It is the denial of one position without clarity of the position on which the objection is based or by which it is warranted. In a word, religious studies should have a basically positive relation to what is studied, and it should be made clear that critiques of religious beliefs and practices that may arise carry with them answers to the questions raised by how, other than religiously, certain human needs and potentials are filled and addressed.

We turn, then, first to an account of the rise of religious studies in the period from the beginning of the nineteenth century to the ending of the twentieth century. This account will be structured by the three shared interests of scholars who in other ways are quite different from one another. Each of the three interests will be put forward as shared by five scholars who are presented in each chapter chronologically. As already mentioned, the scholars included are selected because they illuminate the topic or interest they share, but it is also the case that a department of religious studies should have this or a comparable list of scholarly contributions to the field of religious studies that faculty and students can be counted on to recognize and refer to when discussions about the field arise.

As we move forward, it should be kept in mind that the two parts of the book are affected by the two sources of religious studies, nonreligious and religious. It should also be kept in mind that this book does not advocate the determination of departments of religious studies by either religiously or nonreligiously based interests and objectives but rather suggests that the contributions to religious studies arising from both kinds of interests should be recognized and valued. It is fair to say, however, that this book retains attention to and does not downgrade an emphasis on religious reasons for studying religion. This stance is defensible because a radical change in the ethos of academic culture, and in religious studies, is occurring. It is a change from a generally positive or appreciative view of religion's relation to human well-being to an increasing dependence on materialist assumptions and methods that carry negative consequences for viewing religion. The question that runs through the book, while often only implied, is how and to what extent departments of religious studies can and should put forward religiously identifiable responses to the faults and lacks in late modernity and in academic culture that have become so extensive and corrosive.

The basic or overriding intention of this book, then, is to guide its readers along a path that leads to or adumbrates a greater involvement in one another of religious and nonreligious interests in or approaches to the study of religion. This involvement with one another is based on their shared concern for and attention to human well-being, the interrelations with one another of the humanistic and ethical strain or potential of other academic interests, and the necessary, but certainly not the only or necessarily dominant, relation of religion to human persons, groups, and cultures, a relation grounded in a mutual concern for human well-being.

Part One

HISTORICAL

Chapter 1

MODERNITY, ROMANTICISM, AND THE RISE OF RELIGIOUS STUDIES

The study of religion or, as it has come to be known, religious studies, brings into focus, analyzes, interprets, and evaluates a component of human life that recurs and is often prominent. Interest in it as something to be studied and as something relevant to understanding human cultures, especially those other than Western modernity, became prominent in the late eighteenth and early nineteenth centuries. This does not mean that prior to this time religion in the West was so taken for granted, so naturalized as part of life, and so culturally embedded that it did not draw attention to itself as a discrete object of interest and study. Religion as something particular and distinguishable from other aspects of human life drew attention to itself earlier for several reasons, particularly when it was seen as a cause of social and cultural instability and even conflict. But it can be said that before the middle of the seventeenth century the relation of religion to the daily lives of people was, despite differences and tensions, largely supported by shared cultural assumptions and practices. But after the devastation of the thirty-year war, religion drew attention to itself as a challenge or problem. This justifies the assertion, which one often hears, that "religion" is a modern construction. It could be said, rather, that awareness of religion as a particular factor in human lives and relations that causes differences as well as commonality is largely a modern one. One response to this awareness was to limit the authority and role of religion, especially politically and rationally. While this was an aggravation as well as an antidote to religious conflict, it implied an endorsement of a culture based less on religious beliefs, practices, and institutions and more on what were regarded as shareable advances in human knowledge and control, particularly the economic and political expansion of nations and the advancement of learning, especially in what we now think of as science and technology and their focus on the natural world.

What nations and technology had in common was their associations with power, associations that had as their consequence, intended or not, a diminishing of religion's authority over them. Indeed, religion could be viewed by some as retarding the benefits arising from the increased power of states and the application of science and technology to protect people from threats, whether social or natural, and to extend their control over their surroundings. As political, economic, scientific, and technological power came more to determine the place and role of religion, religion came less to determine how and to what ends power should be used, and power became as much an end as a means. The increasing independence of power and its deployment in service to progress, expansion, and control also meant that Western modernity became oriented less to the past and its perpetuation and more to a future granted by advances largely free from the past and from religious controls and goals. This future orientation derives confirmation from the positive results of advancements in the well-being of larger numbers of people, such as improvements in health care and the deployment of machines able to reduce arduous labor.

Strange as it may appear to say, the roots of these changes can be traced to the sixteenth century and the high value placed, especially by Protestant Christianity, on nature as a storehouse of knowledge, a teacher of wisdom, and an object requiring and deserving close attention. Indeed, nature was viewed as revelation, as a second scripture. While a factor in almost all of Christianity, this high regard for the natural was particularly obvious in Calvinism. A notable and influential figure is Francis Bacon, who took Calvin's theory of reading the Bible and applied it to reading nature as scripture: discovering the principles by which nature is formed, applying those principles to as yet not understood natural phenomena, and striving to lessen threats and obstacles to human well-being. These interests came to be taken as generally available and not dependent on particular religious beliefs. Instead of belief, what was now required was a method of close observation, developing and testing hypotheses, and confirming theories through tangible gains in knowledge and control. The increasing independence and cultural authority of rationality, scientific inquiry, and technology rested both on the obvious gains in knowledge and control of the context of human life and on the applicability of the fruits of knowledge and power largely without regard for religious approval.

The power of nations, as a major factor in the formation of Western modernity, while greatly affected by scientific and technological developments, grew in a less direct way, due in part to the role of religious identities within them. Two factors came particularly to the fore: the religious approbation appropriated by political power, even when concentrated in the hands of a few and exercised at the expense of many, and the development of societies formed by more than one kind of religious identity. These problems were variously resolved, most dramatically but not exclusively, by means of conflict, persecution, and revolution. A major motivation and manifestation of national power was economic, especially entwined with colonial and imperialistic expansion. The extensions of power were also rationally and religiously justified by an interest in discovering the unexplored and impacting the lives of other people in what were generally thought to be beneficial ways. Political and technological powers, while cooperating in many other ways, were similar in treating their contexts as knowable and controllable. Knowledge and discovery were incremental and provided confirmation by means of extension and progress. National extension and the advancements of science and technology were mutually enhancing and carried, for those included in the world widened and secured by them, enormous prestige. The shared cultural benefit of both was to allow people who religiously differed from one another or were not religiously insistent to agree on and participate in common enterprises deemed beneficial. To be thoroughly modern came to be identified with the weakening authority of the past and of religion, the increase in prominence of political and economic determinants, and the extension, by scientific and technological progress, of knowledge and control.

The cultural shift from a religiously derived regard for nature to cultural naturalism or materialism was a less complete process than the increasingly close tie between modernity and the acquisition and deployment of power because nature retained a degree of resistance to control and of value as a teacher of wisdom and object of wonder. Nature has continued as an object of fascination and does so, although compromised, to the present day. Combined with its ready partner, nation, nature came to provide a resource for cultural ideals and for personal, group, and, to some degree, religious identities. Nature and nation, howbeit in differing and at times conflicting ways, continued in modernity to gather and retain religious or religious-like attachments at the expense of religion as a traditional institutional and cultural authority.

Modernity, then, increasingly became a materialist culture by transferring devotion from religious traditions and institutions to nature and nation. The identification of modernity with cultural materialism was abetted by the assumption that what people have in common and can, with a large degree of certainty, speak of or refer to is material. This assumption had two major positive outcomes: it provided the shared basis for intellectual and technological advances, and it gave people a ground that avoids or undercuts religious, cultural, and personal differences. A major but subtle shift caused by the gradual domination in the culture of advancements, particularly in scientific knowledge and technological control and their enhancements of human life, especially manufacturing and agricultural tools, was to give cultural primacy to the extension of physical survival. The boon of alleviating human suffering and extending human survival could be evoked as counterevidence to any critique of modernity one would want to mount.

Crucial to modern progress is a method, generally identified as scientific, for the examination and interpretation of data that has two crucial steps or components, both of which are, incidentally, similar to, if not derived from, Bacon's theory of reading nature as a text. The first is to remove as much as possible from what is studied preconceived understandings and evaluations of it and to view it, as we commonly say, as it is. The second component is to reduce what is studied to its simplest or most basic state, to get behind what appears to what is causal or basic to it and, therefore, primary or more real. This approach to examining and understanding something, while most readily associated with science, was extended from the laboratory out into academic culture more widely, and seeped into common culture. It also had official applications, extending not only to other forms of investigation but to such important social arenas as forensic and judicial practices. Getting beneath what is superficial to uncover what really is the case takes on broad importance, and facts, even when not materially defined, have the standing, by being thought of as separable from and prior to meaning and value, of dependability and truth.

However, the basic method of research is not the only or even primary cause of the formation of a materialist culture. Another and more powerful cause was the increasing effects on personal and corporate life of urbanization, industrialization, and modes of transportation that began noticeably to accelerate at the beginning of the nineteenth century and continue today, when, for example, more than half of the world's population lives in large cities. While these developments and their acceleration can be tied to the role of sovereign nations in determining world order, they extend their effects beyond national boundaries and introduce a new kind of world order, what is sometimes referred to as late modernity, a world order based on the material, especially economic and political, that forms the primary context and means of relations for and between societies. The steadily increasing prominence, even dominance, in Western culture of humanly constructed and controlled contexts and means of human interrelations changed the culture. Human life became increasingly enfolded and determined by external and material constructions that were massive and virtually omnipresent. The external and material came to dominate what is internal or personal in human life; what is physical became more obvious and shared than what is spiritual or moral; what is physical and impersonal became more determining than feelings or responsibilities.

A major response, in the form of exception and resistance, to these developments is one that, however attenuated and diverse, continues into the present day and can loosely be identified as Romanticism, a cultural movement that, beginning in the eighteenth century and accelerating in the nineteenth century, was, among other things, a reaction to the consequences of an advancing materialist culture with an appeal to the personal, internal, natural, spiritual, traditional, and ideal. While there are wide scholarly differences as to what Romanticism was and to what extent it is traceable down to the present, there is general agreement that it was, among other things, a reaction to the culture that had increasingly come into dominance. Three shared emphases among the various forms of Romanticism were, first, a sense of release from constraints, formality, and order; second, a reaffirmation of aspects of human internal life, especially of spiritual, imaginative, and emotional human potentials; and, third, a feeling of correspondence between human, especially personal or internal resources, and nature itself, valued now less for its utility and more for its variety and awesome qualities. These cultural changes, although unorganized, were consistent and compelling enough to form a kind of second and often contrary set of beliefs, orientations, and goals in a culture marked by humanly constructed and controlled environments that are massive, material, interconnected, and impersonal. While the changes in orientations and values did not diminish the impact of a pervasive and powerful materialist context on personal potentials and identities, they opened up an alternative to and an implicit critique of its dominance. Most importantly, they drew attention to and supported human needs, potentials, and desires to which the rising materialist environment could be perceived as indifferent or even threatening. Romanticism heightened the value of exceptions to the dominantly materialist culture, such as gifted individuals like heroes and geniuses, the importance of personal experiences internally registered, and the integrity of ordinary people and their lives, emotions, and environments. The advancing materialist culture was countered by a diversity of exceptions housed broadly under the designation of Romanticism, a cultural movement identifiable less by a unified agenda and more by its contrary relations to what was becoming prominent in the broader culture.

The principal yield of Romanticism, then, was the place and attention given to human potentials and values seen as not included in and by a culture defined increasingly by material, power, rationality, and advance. There arose in the West, therefore, a variously divided culture shaped by such contraries as external and internal, material and spiritual or ideal, massive and personal, constructed and natural, controlled and spontaneous, conforming and unconventional. At the outset of the nineteenth century, a culture of the internal, idealist, spiritual, and natural was able, by means of traditional and institutional ties, to hold its own and even be perceived as the more important of the two. But as the century progressed, the balance shifted, and, if Henry Adams and his assessment of the relation of the Virgin to the Dynamo can be taken as a barometer of this exchange of dominants, the century ended with the culture of the spiritual, internal, ideal, and natural in a defensive stance and, in the ensuing decades, increasingly in retreat. The contrary relations in the academic culture of the first half of the twentieth century between materialism and idealism yielded to what is now the pervasive assumption, one shared increasingly by the wider culture, that what people share, what can be taken with certainty, and what is real are based on and can be traced back not to ideals, spiritual realities, or personal values but to materiality and power. The sedimentary status of materialism in late modern culture is made clear by the fact that people are generally not aware that this assumption largely sets the terms for how they view and act within their world.

The rise of religious studies should be seen, then, in the context of the changing interests, values, and orientations that are at play under the canopy of Romanticism. Religious studies arose in large part as a reaction and antidote to what came to be perceived in the early nineteenth century as increasingly a culture that, for the sake of advancements and their benefits, also created in the culture important faults or deficiencies. Certainly, the study of religion in human life, especially among peoples historically or geographically distant, also arose for reasons related to the culture of inquiry and advancement, particularly the exploration and colonization that brought Europeans increasingly in contact with other peoples and their unfamiliar, sometimes off-putting but also intriguing, behaviors and beliefs. The study of religion was also a part of modernity's rational project to define the human as such and to override national, linguistic, and cultural differences with an understanding of human needs and potentials deemed universal. But what were taken to be the religious beliefs and practices in the many differing cultures encountered—their pervasiveness and their vivid expressions—drew attention to the places and roles of religious beliefs, artifacts, and behaviors in an adequate understanding of human nature. Increasing access to the larger world of human cultures and religions, their vitality, variety, and complexity, provided resources for exposing what the mounting materialist culture of the West lacked. Religions and the study of them exposed shortcomings in modern Western culture and made available resources for reducing or even filling them.

To some degree, it can also be said that the rise of religious studies is in part due to the religious content of Romanticism itself. This content can be indicated primarily as an attempt to make the study of religion relevant to the culture by giving attention to what transcends or is other than human understanding and control and is related to the spiritual potentials and aspects of human life and culture. Whether by its own religious qualities or by fostering interests in the study of human cultures and religions, a major effect of Romanticism was to bring to attention, as a possible antidote for the lacks and faults created by an emerging materialist culture, those resources in the religions and cultures of other peoples deemed relevant to modernity's lacks.

The rise of religious studies was countered by many traditionally religious people, especially Christians, for whom protecting their own religious identities, traditions, and cultural authority seemed more important than recognizing the study of religions as a potential ally in resisting the cultural prominence of materialism. This resistance came somewhat naturally to them because exclusivity and superiority have deep roots in Christianity. From its origins, the question of other religions, even the threat of them, was real. The first question concerned the relations of early Christians to their Jewish identities and context, but as Christianity spread, the question of its standing in relation to Roman power and religions became more urgent. There were various responses to these questions, and we return to some of them later in this guide. Meanwhile, it is fair to say that, with some exceptions, the emphasis fell on difference and distance, especially regarding Greek and Roman religions. The situation became clearer and graver with the onset of the Roman persecution of Christians. However, the situation changed radically in the fourth century. Beginning with Constantine, Christianity changed from being tolerated early in the century until, by the end of the century, it was made the official religion of the Roman empire. Among other results of this radical change in position, the terms of Christianity's relation to other religions were altered so that Christianity became associated with political power that led the way for its relations to other people and their religions, from vulnerability and marginality to superiority and exclusivity.

Attitudes of distance and difference toward other religions were sometimes softened. One cause was the continuing influence of classical thought, especially Platonic, on Christian theology and its supplementation in the high Middle Ages by the prominence of Aristotle and, perhaps even more interestingly, Aristotle by way of Islamic sources. This role of classical content in medieval Christian culture was carried forward by the Enlightenment, and its emphasis on rationality as a human-making characteristic supported the advance of rational and scientific knowledge that provided a rationale for the elevation of modern Western culture above other cultures construed as not only different but also as rationally and culturally underdeveloped and inferior. Christianity, meanwhile, had a history of its own that prepared people for an appreciative interest in and study of the religions of other cultures.

The rise of religious studies, although resisted and even countered by Christian interests and institutions on the one side and by an academic culture increasingly identified with materialist assumptions and methods on the other, derived cultural support from Romanticism. Like Romanticism generally, religious studies shared an implicit critique of the increasing cultural orientation toward materialism, primarily by turning attention to deficiencies caused by neglect or repression of important human needs and potentials. Romanticism, in addition to having some degree of religious content of its own, contributed, by its general emphasis on human feelings and emotions, to important shifts within Christian interests themselves, especially based on personal experience, that were relevant to Pietism and revivalism. As M. H. Abrams points out, Romanticism carried religious content that construed religious interests in human terms, and many other scholars have exposed religious ingredients in Romanticism. But for our purposes, it is less important to establish Romanticism as itself a religious phenomenon than to recognize it as culturally larger than but related to and supportive of the rise of the study of religion as we know it today.[1]

Two things are implicit in the move from a culture increasingly determined by the construction of massive and inclusive material conditions to what lies beyond the boundaries of that construction in other cultures, past or distant. First was the tacit recognition that materialism, as determining not only a method but also a way of life, could not be stopped or altered. There was a dynamic to the processes of urbanization, industrialization, transportation, and communication that was itself a demonstration, if not a validation, of the implicit agenda behind them. These developments had a defining force and direction that modern culture was as much determined by as it was responsible for. Despite disruptions and conflicts, the general cultural direction seemed to be advancement. The argument for materialist assumptions is its claim to tangible and, to a large degree, beneficial results. Oppositions and alternatives to it have to be advocated on less tangible or agreed-upon grounds and relate more to the past than to the future and more to what is missing or suppressed than to what is visible and operative. The second was the recognition that the primary contraries to materialism would be provided not by countering it but by supplements or compensations for it.

---

[1] See especially M. H. Abrams, *Natural Supernaturalism: Tradition and Revolution in Romantic Literature* (New York: W. W. Norton and Co., 1971). See also, e.g., Bernard M.G. Reardon, *Religion in the Age of Romanticism* (Cambridge: Cambridge University Press, 1985), J. Robert Barth, S.J., *Coleridge and Christian Doctrine* (Cambridge, MA: Harvard University Press, 1969), and Jeffrey W. Barbeau, ed., *Coleridge's Assertion of Religion: Essays on the Opus Maximum* (Leuven: Peeters, 2006).

The most that could be done was to point out that materialism, both as a theory and as a way of living, was deficient because it produced a culture not only of gains but also of lacks and faults. The sources of additions and supplements to that culture were many: theoretical idealism, attentive regard for nature, art, and the creative imagination; admiration for extraordinary or creative people such as political leaders, prophets, and heroes; and the realm of human internality, especially feelings and emotions. These sources created the divided culture we have grown to take for granted, namely, a culture determined by massive, shared, and external material conditions on the one side and a culture attentive to human values, feelings, and creative achievements, often related to or expressed by religious language and practices, on the other. The two cultures or aspects of modernity, while distinguishable from and often contrary to one another, at times join, primarily where individual creativity and even heroism are tied to significant scientific, technological, economic, and political developments. However, despite occasional crossovers or coincidences between the two—the internal and the external, the ideal and the material, and the personal and the public—they began to form contrary spheres and divided identities.

Studying religion, then, was one of the ways to identify, amplify, and confirm the realm that stood as an exception, correction, or supplement to the rising materialist culture. More importantly, it assumed a mediating position between the emerging contraries because, while it drew attention to religion, it did so in a scholarly and even scientifically recognizable way and made available data concerning human needs and potentials that suggested universality by being globally extensive and historically deep. An implicit case was made, namely, that there was something not only pervasive in human life but also human-making that was formed in response to something more or other than what could be understood or controlled. The rich variety and vitality of what came to be housed under the category of religion was itself arresting, and the extent, variety, and force of it seemed significant even in the face of modernity's materialist determinants. A major, although largely implicit, goal in the rise of religious studies was to address the lacks and faults created by modernity's identification with the material and the advancement of human knowledge, constructions, and control and to do this in recognizably academic and scholarly ways.

Among the cultural faults or lacks caused by or resulting from the advances of modernity, three can be seen as prominent and recurring in the research and theories of otherwise diverse scholars from the early nineteenth century and into the present century. A relation is detectable between cultural deficiencies perceived as caused by the course and conditions of modernity and what was taken by them as particularly interesting or even definitive in the religious peoples studied. Representative scholars shared a sense of the relevance of the religions in the cultures they studied to the lacks or faults in modernity.

One of these lacks is the failure of the increasingly dominant culture adequately to take into account, to neglect, and even to repress, resources left behind or marginalized by a cultural preoccupation with advancement, resources basic to human life and needed for enriching, revitalizing, and correcting it. This lack is created by a culture primarily oriented toward the advancement of power and control.

The second lack or fault is the loss of access to personal and group experiences and relationships that people need for their well-being, both as communities and as individuals, experiences and relationships that are, in contrast to the material, intangible. Religious beliefs and practices are studied for their potential in providing access to these needed resources.

A third perceived lack or fault is the inability of a materialistically determined culture to provide people with an adequate worldview. Materialism could not provide an adequate sense of living in a meaningful world and of relations within and to it that are fulfilling and personally and socially warranting.

In the following chapters, then, each of these three lacks or interests will be treated in relation to five scholars of religion who, among other matters as important or even more important in their work, draw attention to one of these lacks, faults, or needs and the ways in which religion can or does address it. This does not mean that the three cultural lacks or faults and the characteristics of religion that each group of scholars, in their various ways, bring to attention are exhaustive or defining of their work, of religious studies more broadly considered, or of the course and nature of religious studies today. But the three lacks and the responses to them are comprehensive, complex, and elastic enough to support the suggestion that they continue to be relevant to human life and culture today. Religious studies should continue to address these and other interests in the present because a materialist culture does not adequately address them. They continue to need addressing for the fulfillment of human needs, the actualization of human potentials, and the realization of the goals of human well-being. The scholars chosen as examples of giving attention to each of these three lacks or interests and their recurring and continuing importance for religious studies are chronologically treated from the early nineteenth century into the present century. The implied argument is that the study of religion as we know it in the present day can be taken as a line of inquiry, knowledge, and concern that is well established and worthy of extension and augmentation. Implied, too, is the suggestion that the three topics and the interests of selected scholars in them are not exceptions but examples of a broad and complex but also identifiable current of inquiry that has been and continues to be culturally relevant and academically engaging. While other lacks and faults in the culture and the corrective or healing contributions of religion to them, as well as scholars interested in them, could be added to or substituted for those here gathered, it is hoped that these will serve to offer an answer to questions concerning the origins, coherence, and continuing relevance religion and studying it have to personal, social, and cultural needs and potentials.

It is also important to notice and keep in mind, as we trace these shared or recurring interests in the work of fifteen selected scholars, that they are professionally located in nonreligious faculties and have academic interests located primarily in the social or human sciences. This does not mean, however, that they treat religion as something to be subjected to or explained by nonreligious interests or methods. Religion, although variously understood and treated, is generally taken by them as something both particular and relevant to human life and cultures. It also should be kept in mind that they bring to attention what in religion is not taken to be relevant to modernity but also addresses what they see as its needs and faults. They share a critical or diagnostic as well as a remedial or corrective interest in what in the religion they study is relevant to modernity.

Finally, it should be kept in mind that this historical treatment of recurring interests in the study of religion is not the only source of religious studies as we have come to recognize it. As put forward in the Introduction, it is one of two sources. The second was a detectable cultural shift in the mid-twentieth century, especially in the United States, toward the place and role of religion itself in religious studies and its relation to personal, social, and even political life. The cultural conditions of that time gave rise to an interest in restoring to American culture a religious ingredient or element that should be part of public as well as personal or group identity. We shall look at this second source in the second part of this book, although we shall do so in a way that is less specific and particular and more implicit and complex in its effects on religious studies today than was the case a half century ago.

Chapter 2

STUDYING RELIGION AND CULTURAL FAULTS CAUSED BY REPRESSION AND NEGLECT

We turn now to describing the first of two sources for the formation of religious studies as we now know it, namely, a noticeable, sustained, and generally positive rise of academic interest in the religion of various peoples, especially those distant both historically and geographically from modern Western culture. Two factors contributed to this interest. The first and more obvious stimulus was the accumulation of reports from the wide and vigorous explorations of distant places and their peoples that were mainly a byproduct of the political and economic interests behind them. Among the characteristics of these many cultures was the shared importance of religion for them. The prominence of religion gave otherwise distant cultures a shared constant and cultural relation to Western modernity, in which religion was also a continuing factor. A second motivation, as already discussed, was the increasingly materialist quality of Western modernity and the increasing role of environments humanly designed and controlled, primarily industrialization, urbanization, and the mobility created by new forms of transportation. Closely related to this characteristic of modernity was a shift in cultural orientation from the authority of the past to the lure of the future and advancement. Differing or distant cultures, in contrast, were seen as having respect for what preceded human constructions and a regard for the non-material. The study of religion, then, was related to the more general awareness in Romanticism of earlier and other cultures, ordinary human life, human emotions, relations with nature, and the importance of the non-material or spiritual. The study of religion can be seen, then, as an occasion to bring to attention human needs and potentials that had lost centrality in Western modernity and even neglected or repressed by the advancing culture of material construction and human control. However, the study of distant people, it should be noticed, was also made possible by technological advancements that enabled explorers, colonists, and missionaries to reach distant and unfamiliar places and peoples. This fact created a noticeable degree of ambivalence in the work of these scholars.

One of the interests in or results of studying other cultures and religions, then, was to call attention to human needs and potentials that Western culture could be seen, when contrasted with the cultures encountered, as undervaluing. The prominence in modernity of the future and the advancement of knowledge and human control implied a corresponding neglect of the past and of what preceded or under-girded human understandings and constructions. A byproduct of a culture oriented toward intellectual and technological advancement and a sense of growing distance between a future-oriented present and the past was an awareness that matters important for human well-being were receiving less attention and regard than they deserved.

We turn, then, to five examples of scholars whose studies of religion, though in many respects very different from one another, reveal a shared awareness of and appreciation for the role of religion in retaining and evoking the significance and standing of the past and of values neglected or repressed in a culture increasingly determined by advancing human understanding, construction, and control. We shall look at the examples in chronological order, thereby tracing a line of continuing and shared interest in religious studies that is relevant yet today.

J. J. Bachofen (1815–1887)[1]

Bachofen is important for this topic or interest in religious studies because he exposed, mostly indirectly, what a culture defined by advancement in power and control almost inevitably neglects and even represses. His work implies that a culture dominated by what humans construct and control, although not necessarily by intention, takes what is otherwise primary and causal and relegates it to a secondary, overshadowed, or superseded status.

Bachofen was a historian who studied Greco-Roman antiquity, particularly Roman law, at the University of Basel, where he taught. A controlling conviction within his studies of antiquity is that behind the advancing patriarchal cultures of Athens and Rome, there existed earlier and repressed forms of social organization that were noticeably matriarchal. The evidence he puts forward in defense of this theory is drawn mainly from his study of the Lycians, an early civilization in Western Asia Minor.

---

[1] For this section, see especially J. J. Bachofen, *Myth, Religion, and Mother Right* (Princeton: Princeton University Press, 1967), pp. 69–115.

Bachofen isolates several traces of an earlier civilization that he took as indications of a matriarchal social order. One is that children are given names that tied them to their mothers' families, and family histories and identities were established and traced through maternal lines. More importantly, daughters rather than sons inherited the family goods and were responsible for preserving the family traditions. He draws attention to other cultures as bearing traces of these characteristics, such as Egypt, and, indeed, his conclusions may well be more expansive than the evidence he puts forward warrants. He implies that matriarchal qualities in early societies were not exceptional but widespread. His implied defense for building a larger case for his theory than is established by evidence seems to be that patriarchal societies, with their goals of advancement and achievement, can be expected to neglect, forget, or repress the importance of earlier and matriarchal social formations.

Bachofen offers additional support for his hypothesis by pointing to vestiges of earlier matriarchal societies that remain after they are replaced by patriarchy, aspects that persist, such as a fascination for the moon and for the night in general, the sanctity of mother love and nurture, attention to, even reverence for, the dead and the realm of the dead, the special meanings and powers associated with the left or weaker hand, and the high value placed on birth, renewal, and reconciliation.

Another point of Bachofen, one that he could possibly have made more of, is that a matriarchal order healed a social condition that he called Hetaerism, an original social disorder he posits as marked by promiscuity and the confusion of family ties. A matriarchal order could replace this chaotic situation with the relative certainty of identifying children with their mothers, a phenomenon duplicated in much of the animal kingdom. His argument for early matriarchal social and cultural formations in this and other ways implies an appeal to natural patterns.

His argument for the natural origins of social order is given resonance in Bachofen by his use of the term "mystery" to refer both to the events of pregnancy and birth and to the nurturing of their young by mothers. This move gives an added dimension to the significance of what lies below or is left behind by patriarchal societies when they replace and repress matriarchal order with patriarchal order. By identifying itself with knowledge, power, and advance, a patriarchal social order reveals impatience with mystery and its larger role in matriarchy, making knowledge, control, and distinctions primary at the expense of the "mysteries" associated with reproduction, early nurture, and the similarities between human relations and the wider natural scene.

In relation to his point about an earlier and repressed matriarchal social order, Bachofen deploys a theory of language. He posits symbolic language, which holds contraries in relation to one another, as primary relative to literal language, which particularizes and categorizes. He saw symbolic language as basic to myth, which relates symbols to one another and provides, especially by means of narrative, a unified world. In a patriarchal society, myths are replaced by histories, particularly accounts of human achievements and progress, eventually denigrating myth to a secondary and even outmoded position relative to history.

It is clear that Bachofen, like other scholars of early societies that we shall discuss in this chapter, makes being more important than becoming, relations more important than distinctions, and caring more important than control. He was working at a time when, in academic culture, the history of human advancement was increasingly prominent in the human sciences. His argument amounted, then, to a reversal of priorities and values. What was taken as advance could be viewed as neglectful and repressive in its failure adequately to take into account aspects of human life that in earlier social forms were more highly valued. He sets up a contrary relation between cultures marked by relationships, caring, myth-making, and mystery and those marked by distinctions, law, history writing, and control. The study of religion, then, becomes an apology, however implicit, for a social order with interests contrary to those of modernity, an apology that suggests a loss in modern culture of the primary status and role of realities and values more fully associated with matriarchy.

With Bachofen, the study of earlier cultures and their religions in the context of an academic culture oriented to knowledge gained in order to control carries an implied cultural critique by exposing the priorities of other and earlier cultures and their diminished roles in modernist contexts. The study of earlier cultures, then, draws attention to realities, kinds of people, and human values that modernity slights or even represses. It could be suggested that Bachofen extends the conclusions he draws from the somewhat limited evidence he cites because of his implied critique of modernity as a culture inclined to estimate earlier cultures as inferior and to consider research directed toward them as of questionable worth. In any case, an implied consequence of his theories is to reveal the negative relations not only of Greek and Roman cultures to the matriarchal base from which they arose but also the replication by modern culture of such neglectful or repressive acts. He implies that the study of early cultures and religions counters the assumptions and effects of modern, including academic, culture. His work calls into question a culture or social order that gives precedence to human power, advancement, and control at the expense of the place and role in human life of what is primary, generative, unifying, nurturing, and renewing.

F. Max Müller (1823–1900)[2]

While Bachofen could easily be overlooked when selecting examples with which to trace themes and interests in the emergence of religious studies, that would not be the case for Max Müller. He made a substantial, two-pronged contribution to the methodology of religious studies, namely, accessibility to primary texts and the comparative method. The status of these two contributions has endured, and Müller continues to hold a place in debates concerning methods and resources for studying religion. Although with a very different emphasis, he shares with Bachofen a concern for what value is left behind when attention is turned to human advancements in knowledge and control.

Educated in Germany, Müller moved to Oxford in his early twenties and spent his academic career there. He was both a philosopher and a comparative philologist, with particular interest in Sanskrit. He translated ancient Hindu texts and was principally responsible for the production of *The Sacred Books of the East* (1879), which provided scholars with primary texts of Eastern religious traditions. In addition, he applied the methods of comparative linguistics to the study of religions, arguing that comparison can reveal, as it does when languages are compared, the similarities and differences between religions and, especially relative to similarities, the pervasive and persistent role of religion in human life. The ensuing and enduring importance of textuality and the comparative method for the development of religious studies is an important story in itself.

Himself a practicing Christian, Müller was well aware of the threats that a comparative study of religions poses for adherents of a particular religion. Religious people who are asked to view religiously different peoples appreciatively will not readily consider their own religion as standing alongside others under a general category and being treated equally with them. While he did not solve the problem raised by the relations of one's own religious identity to the understanding and even appreciation of other religions, he showed by example that a personal religious identity and a positive orientation toward other religions need not conflict with one another. The problem he addressed as a religious person and as a scholar is not, even today, wholly resolved, and we shall return to it in the second part of this guide. Müller contended that the broadening effect of a comparative approach need not dilute one's religious identity, that depth is not necessarily

---

2 For this section, see especially F. Max Müller, *Introduction to the Science of Religion* (London: Longmans, Green, and Co., 1893), pp. 3–23 and 196–207.

lost in breadth, and that the risks involved in considering appreciatively the religions of others do not outweigh the advantages.

Müller's other methodological stress, the importance of early texts for the study of a religion, has a recognizable Protestant ring to it. He imputed primacy in a religion not to its later developments or present manifestations but to its earliest stages. The study of a religion, then, should contrast its early and later forms, viewing the latter as less important than the earlier. This conforms to the emphasis of the Reformers in Christian history, who considered later developments in the Church, which in Catholicism are more highly valued, as needing to be held in question in order to give primary attention to the earliest forms of Christianity, particularly biblical texts read in their original languages. The distinction to be made between the less and the more valuable in a tradition was not for Müller so much a distinction between true and false or orthodox and heretical as between more and less clear or pure. In addition to its conformity with the Protestant principle of evaluating later manifestations in light of Christianity's earliest forms, his emphasis on founding texts and on religious origins, which we will encounter in other scholars, also appeals, from a Romantic viewpoint, to individual genius and leadership. Müller took religious founders to be persons motivated by their thirst for truth and for living exemplary lives.

Müller's principal hypothesis concerning the source or base of religion in human life is that the human mind has within it an awareness of and a fascination for the Infinite. The primary source from which this human capacity for the Infinite draws confirmation is nature, especially due to their vastness and power, the sky and the sun. Religion develops when people identify the Infinite with particular, especially celestial, realities, give it names, and begin to relate to what is named as though it were a personal being. While almost inevitable, this process for Müller carries a cost because it eventually neglects or represses the distinction between the derivative particulars and the Infinite as primary or original. Indeed, he sees this inevitable, or at least recurring, neglect as a kind of Fall. The exchange is unfortunate not only because it overvalues the particular but also because it dulls the inherent capacity of the human mind to affirm and appreciate the Infinite. This emphasis in Müller exposes, incidentally, the basis of his contention that one can identify with a particular religion and yet understand and appreciate other religions because a person has the capacity, which Müller values as a human-making characteristic, to keep from exchanging the Infinite for the particulars of a religion, including one's own.

One can see in Müller's emphasis on human capacity and desire for the Infinite some similarity to idealism generally and to Kant particularly, especially Kant's emphasis on the conditions or forms of reason which cannot themselves be thought. Müller's point also bears some similarity to later developments in linguistics, especially those commonly referred to as structuralist, theories that posit an underlying mental structure that determines linguistic formation and other patterns of human behaviors. It also bears some similarity with theories of recent cognitive scientists who posit a mental capacity for the transcendent, as though the human mind is hardwired to take the Infinite into account.

Despite its importance for understanding Müller, his contribution concerning the human capacity for affirming the Infinite is less acknowledged today than his translation of ancient texts that made available to Western scholars a large body of invaluable material. He prized religious texts for making possible what he called a "science" of religion. These texts formed a common basis for scholars to come to agreement about particular religions, about the ways in which earlier and later stages of a religious tradition can be distinguished, and about the similarities and differences between religions. The availability of ancient texts and the understanding of religions when compared with one another, which the accessibility of texts makes possible, is not finally what is most important for Müller, however. Most important for him is what precedes not only texts but language itself, namely, the human capacity for and apprehension of the Infinite. This capacity forms the point from which the texts, beliefs, and practices of particular religions should be viewed.

Müller's work, then, is relevant to the ongoing discussion among scholars of religion concerning the status of texts and textuality. At the most obvious level, this discussion swirls around the fact that influential scholars of religion such as Müller were Protestants and, therefore, strongly inclined to give their attention to what could be called the scriptures of religions. Scholars affected by or attentive to other forms of Christianity and to other religions may well contend that texts and beliefs are not to be taken as universally central and that practices, objects, and other more visible characteristics of religious life are as, if not more, important. The questioning of methods shaped by the predominantly Protestant milieu for the rise of religious studies carries with it a suspicion of the legitimacy for studying religion of an emphasis on texts and the beliefs derived from, or doctrinal interpretations of, them. This critique reminds us that, while oral and written texts in a religious tradition may contribute greatly to a scholar's understanding of it, one cannot impute to all religions and to religion itself the importance that the texts of a religion have for the scholar.

Like the category of the mysterious in Bachofen, Müller relates religion in its basic and generative form to the human capacity for something prior or transcendent to human knowledge and constructions. Like Bachofen, too, he sees the development of culture as a kind of Fall. For Müller, exchanging the Infinite for something particular and the Fall-like consequences of doing so can only be avoided by reaffirming the unique force and significance of the Infinite that religions carry, if only as a vestige or obscured potential, within or behind them. The study of religions, then, involves, along with much else for him, a recovery of the human-making characteristic to apprehend and to be oriented by the Infinite, an appreciation for a human capacity that precedes, transcends, and critiques human constructions, including language and even religion itself.

It is useful to point out, finally, what should be obvious in Müller's work, namely, its connections with recurring and prominent interests in Romanticism. One of them is his attention to religious founders as individuals who bring to awareness human capacities that lie as latent potential in humanity generally. Another is his turning to nature, especially the sun, as the first and most obvious source of identification with the Infinite in human recognition. A third is his emphasis on the pre-linguistic as the seat of human wholeness, of something unspoken that gives rise to language and upon which human understanding and control depend. Finally, there are the traces of philosophical Idealism, especially the primary role in human awareness of the capacity for the Infinite. In general, we can see in his work an example of referring to something basic and enabling that stands prior to human understanding and control and that is obscured by the progressively and materialistically oriented culture in which he is working.

James G. Frazer (1854–1941)[3]

While it would be a mistake to identify the work of James Frazer primarily as making an awareness and study of early and distant forms of religion culturally popular, it is true that he is largely responsible for disseminating an awareness of, even a fascination for, early and non-Western religions among the general literate public. There is, to put it roughly, a relation between his work and the appearance by the middle of the twentieth century of coffee-table books on religious myths and symbols in the homes of people wanting to keep up with what culturally is innovative and unusual.

Frazer was a Cambridge University anthropologist, and he developed a wide knowledge of religions. But he made the subject available to people because he stressed similarities between religious beliefs and practices across

---

3 For this section, see especially James George Frazer, *The Golden Bough: A Study in Magic and Religion*, one volume abridged edition (New York: Macmillan Publishing Company, 1922), pp. 1–12.

cultural distinctions, suggesting that behind the diversity of religions there exist common elements that make taking an interest in religions less difficult than it might otherwise have seemed. In addition, he was a gifted writer, so that his major work, *The Golden Bough*, which was published over the decade from 1913 to 1924 and comprised twelve volumes, remains a literary as well as an anthropological achievement.

Frazer was an armchair anthropologist who depended for his material primarily on the reports of others, such as explorers, missionaries, and colonists. This physical distance from the actual particularities of religious practices may well have supported his thesis that there are common elements in religions and that a comparative view of them allowed for the formation of a relatively unified account. This means that his work had both a breadth of range and an inclusiveness of theory. Important to his theory is that religions, rather than having at their outset, as argued by the examples already treated, a more positive stage, had desire and even violence as their originating base.

While the energy and violence of the early stages in religious development gave Frazer's readers an access to something fascinating beneath or behind religion as it presented itself in its more institutional and rational forms, that energy, while intriguing, also warranted modifications introduced as religions developed. Frazer posited three stages in religious development, a magical stage, which was the most violent, a religious stage that emphasized particular deities and was marked by greater order, and the present stage, a rational stage from which to view religion as largely surpassed and outmoded.

Because the primary characteristics of religion are shared, Frazer deemed it legitimate to describe individual practices as synecdoches of the whole. The most well-known of his examples provides the title of his major work. The setting of his narrative is the Italian town of Aricia and the nearby Lake of Nemi, the site of an ancient temple to Diana, the goddess associated with hunting and, more importantly, with fertility and childbirth. Located in the wood near the lake was a sacred tree that had a golden branch. If someone could get hold of this branch, that person was empowered to kill and replace the priest/king. The rise, fall, and replacement of the priest/king forms a pattern related to fertility. Religion, as we recognize it today, is the vestige of an original and violent pattern of exchange and renewal. While the later ordering of religion makes religion more acceptable because it replaces earlier violence, it also allows religions to look for alternative or substitute victims or to institutionalize repression. The line of human development, from brutality to religion and from religion to rationality, while an advance, also exposes a fault or creates a lack.

It is not the case that, for Frazer, the stages of development in religions are wholly discrete from one another. For example, he viewed the magical stage as marked by a degree of rational order, specifically the two laws of magic. The first is the law of similarity, which holds that similar things can affect one another, as the act of pouring water can affect rainfall. The second is the law of contact, which holds that things once connected can, though separated, still affect one another. It can be said that the first law is metaphoric and the second is metonymic.

The religious stage evolves not only in response to the disorder of the magical stage but also because the earlier stage often failed to produce the desired results that more sophisticated people desired. Therefore, belief in deities arose, particularly related to various human potentials and needs, deities from whom recognition and results could be sought.

The rational stage arises when humans develop sufficient confidence in their own knowledge and skills to address their needs and fulfill their desires. This pattern of human development seems to parallel Frazer's personal path from the Presbyterianism of his youth to the atheism of his adulthood. He came to view religious practices in his own day as vestiges from earlier stages of human development. One could see these vestiges in the beliefs and practices of rural people who maintain recognizable ties with early religion, in some forms of Christianity, especially Roman Catholicism, and in the authority that people continue to confer on kings and priests. This reliance of religion in the present time on superseded stages gives cultural advancement continuity in addition to change, indicating, as did also his emphasis on similarity as well as differences between religions, the need of the human mind for unity and continuity as well as diversity and change.

While Frazer posed the present as an advance on the past, a present with which he identified, he also exposed in his extended and various accounts of religions a vital sub-stratum in human life. This contributed to giving a new kind of value to the so-called primitive in high modernity. The importance of myth and ritual as literary tropes provided a culture that was, by virtue of urbanization, industrialization, and developing forms of transportation and communication, becoming humanly controlled but also uncentered, a sense of basic and shared human patterns and vitality were available to Frazer's contemporaries more by reading his work than by the religious beliefs and practices his work described. It also gave to readers of his work a sense of knowing more fully than their religious neighbors what religion came out of, still contained, and primarily was about. He attributed to those who study religion, then, a degree of cultural advantage over those in the culture who continued to self-identify as religious persons. His readers could take an interest in religion and even view some aspects of it appreciatively, while also justifying their separation from it. The study of religion provided a culture marked by the uprooting of people and the disruptions of cultural continuity, an awareness of something embedded in human history and memory that all people, despite their differences, do or can share. And Frazer articulated what easily can be felt by a culture that has become more rational, scientific, and technological, namely, the appeal of human vitality, spontaneity, and disruption, potentials in human life that, it can be added, were of importance for Romanticism.

Frazer, then, exemplifies an ambivalence regarding religion's continuing interest, an ambivalence that at times can be found among those engaged today in the study of religion. The negative view of religion as a stage in human advancement that needs to be superseded was becoming an established and widespread opinion in academic culture. But a counter evaluation, related to Romanticism, continued, namely, that the study of religion gives a person contact with something important and fascinating behind or below modern, particularly rationalist, materialist, and technological, culture and its constructions, without requiring the student of religion to self-identify or be regarded as being religious. Studying religion became a way of deriving some benefits from religion without being identified with it. In this, the scholar of religion has the support and company of a range of artists in high and later modernity who could, thanks to Frazer and others, enrich and vitalize their work in a similar way.

Carl Gustav Jung (1875–1961)[4]

Carl Jung, like Frazer and Sigmund Freud, at whom we shall look later, influenced several areas of cultural and academic interest, including literary studies. Like them, too, his influence arose from his theory of the roles of myths and ancient stories in conveying dynamics deeply embedded in internal human life and humanly shared. As there arose a Freudian form of literary theory and criticism, so also there arose a Jungian form, an emphasis on the role of myths in literature, as in the influential work of Northrop Frye, Joseph Campbell, Philip Rahv, and other so-called myth critics. The difference between Frazer and Freud, on the one hand, and Jung, on the other, however, was that in the former what precedes modern cultural advancements, while intriguing, is being, or needs to be, superseded. Jung's emphasis, in contrast, is on the continuing positive

---

4 For this section, see especially Carl Gustav Jung, *Psychology and Religion* (New Haven: Yale University Press, 1938), pp. 1–9 and 70–77.

roles of the unconscious in human life, and his primary interest, similar to Bachofen's, was in myths and symbols that concerned maternal matters, birth, nurture, and renewal.

Although Jung was a student of Native American and traditional African religions and traveled to both locations for his investigations, he is known primarily as a psychologist and held a professorship in psychology at the University of Zurich. He is also known as being an associate of Freud from 1907 until 1913. His work continues to be extended by the Jung Institute in Zurich, which was founded in 1948.

Jung, with his more positive view of the unconscious and religion, thought of ancient myths and symbols as having continued relevance to human formation and psychic health. This theory was widely convincing, and he developed a public as well as an academic audience. Like Frazer, he also emphasized similarities between the myths and symbols of diverse cultures, and he gave to the study of religion at least the appearance of an empirical base. He also made religion an inclusive category related not only to early or distant but also to current Western cultures.

Jung, like Freud, turned his attention primarily to the unconscious, but rather than seeing it as a hotbed of impulses and drives, in other words as energy, he saw it as an organizing, meaning-giving, and renewing structure. This positive view of the unconscious was strengthened by Jung's theory that the structuring potential of the unconscious was humanly shared, so that people, however much they differ from one another, also form, to use a term closely associated with Jung, a "collective." He saw the affects of the generative and structuring unconscious not only in religion but also in art and other imaginative expressions. The unifying, renewing, and meaning-granting unconscious is a humanly shared personal and cultural support. This means that religious beliefs and practices have their source not primarily in the conscious designs of people but in something that comes or is revealed to them. What arises from the unconscious is what gives coherence, renewal, and direction to human life and has the quality of being a gift.

Like Freud, Jung also turned to dreams as sites of the force and significance of the unconscious, but he related dreams not so much to repressed desires and drives as to primordial myths and symbols. Such myths and symbols can be read as arising from the archetypes of the collective unconscious. Jung posited components of this collective, such as the number 4, which provides a recurring structure for cosmological myths, the mother figure or anima, which serves as a source of nurture and renewal, and the journey of the hero. The pattern of the hero's journey was particularly useful for literary, especially narrative, theory and criticism. It unified the stories of heroes who enter an unknown and even forbidding realm, seize a boon, and undergo a harrowing return with it, and it related narrative plots to the psychic, often difficult, journey of consciousness into the unconscious and receiving the boon of renewal primarily given by the primal mother figure.

While Jung viewed religion positively and in ways that supported the claims of religious people that their interests were due to revelation and the transcendent, Jung saw the transcendent as existing in the unconscious level of the human psyche. In this, he differed from other theorists who based their views of religious experience on something outside oneself, such as William James and Rudolf Otto. Since the unconscious is, by Jung's definition, beyond cognitive grasp, its nature and even existence must be inferred or hypothesized. If this is true of the unconscious in a person, it is even more true of the unconscious as a universal or collective structure revealed by the appearance of archetypes. While Jung's theories carry some similarities to those of Bachofen, who also saw a life-giving and nurturing maternal reality behind or below repressive paternal motives and structures, Jung located this substratum and its universality primarily as an unchanging psychic rather than as a historical or social reality. Theorists of this kind, despite their differences, identify religion not with something conscious, various, or occasional in human life but with something primal, generative, and essentially human, something that increased rationality and control in modern culture unfortunately tends to undervalue, neglect, or repress in favor of conscious human capacities, designs, and agency.

Although the influence and popularity of Jung has diminished since its peak in the middle decades of the twentieth century, it lingers. And it does, perhaps, because his view of human internality not as a dynamo of needs and desires but as a meaning-granting and renewing resource, gives people a potential that is not only positive but also both individualized and shared. The process of becoming a more meaningful and directed self is related to, rather than countered by, religion. Since for Jung the collective unconscious is made available not only in religious symbols and myths but also in a culture's art, his work gives a positive and substantial account of the relation of religion, art, and other cultural interests that together existed in a parallel, if not contrary, relation to the dominantly materialist characteristics of modern culture. The enduring influence of Jung and other theorists of religion who focus on human internality and experience is based on the continuing fascination for the authority of what is neglected or repressed by modernity in its dominant orientation to understanding and control. Religious studies and theories of the role of religion in reaffirming what modern culture represses, neglects, or marginalizes constitute a remedial response to modernity's lacks and reveal ties to Romanticism that persist.

Victor Turner (1920–1983)[5]

The final theorist at whom we shall look as an example of studying religion as a way of identifying and retrieving what is primary and even crucial for human well-being but has been neglected or repressed by modern culture is Victor Turner. Born in Glasgow, Scotland, he studied classics at the University of London and, after the Second World War, traveled to Zambia to study traditional societies. Unlike some of the theorists at whom we have looked, he focused less on myths, symbols, and beliefs and more on rituals, their patterns and their roles in society. This focus may well be due to the fact that his mother was an actress and a founding member of the Scottish National Theatre, which gave Turner an early exposure to performance. He received his doctoral degree from the University of Manchester in 1955, and, after teaching there, he moved to Stanford University in 1961, to Cornell University in 1964, to the University of Chicago in 1968, and to the University of Virginia in 1978. It is interesting to note that at Virginia he turned his attention increasingly away from the rituals of traditional societies and to performance theory more generally, including recent experimental theater.

Turner is known, therefore, primarily as a theorist of rituals, and that has given his work a currency that continues to the present because of the increasingly important place of ritual and performance theory in religious studies. One basis of Turner's theory of ritual is the work of Arnold van Gennep, particularly van Gennep's theory of the threefold structure of rites of passage: separation from the established social structure, entry into a state that, by its disorder or deprivation, has few if any characteristics of the first stage, and a reincorporation into the social structure in which the initiate is given new rights and obligations. This pattern holds some similarity, we should note, to the journey of the hero in Jung.

Turner gave particular attention to the second stage in the ritual process, one that the initiate or practitioner enters upon leaving the ordinary or structured world. This stage holds a contrary relation to that which the initiate or practitioner leaves behind and reenters at the conclusion of the ritual. The term Turner uses to indicate this middle stage is liminality, and it is more unlike the other two stages in the ritual process than the other stages are unlike one another. The liminal stage is associated with non-differentiation, equality, and unformed potential. The first and third stages are associated with distinctions, structure, and inequality. The liminal brings the high down to the low and the formed down to the potential from which it arises.

---

5 For this section, see especially Victor W. Turner, *The Ritual Process: Structure and Anti-Structure* (Chicago: Aldine Publishing Company, 1966), pp. 94–113 and 125–130.

In the liminal stage, the initiate or practitioner is passive and impressionable, divested of individuality and identity, and exposed to the potentials that give rise to society's structures and order. More broadly, the liminal stage reminds the whole society that its constructions are partial relative to the resources that precede them and are entered in the second stage of the ritual process. Individuals, including rulers, are humbled, realizing that their powers, while related to themselves and the community, come from a source that lies behind or below them. Turner sets up a list of contraries between the liminal stage and the forms and characteristics of personal and communal life in the first and third stages, such as nakedness or uniform clothing vs. distinctions of clothing, sexuality vs. sexual abstinence, disregard for rank vs. distinctions of rank, and the sacred vs. the secular.

In more highly developed societies, the liminal stage is institutionalized, as in the monastic life of Medieval Europe or in mendicant existence. And it can be found more generally in the position of weak, minority, or marginal figures or groups within a society: jesters, misfits, gypsies, and the like, as they variously appear in societies or in their literature. These outside or disenfranchised figures are often associated with moral value or with uncanny powers, such as telling fortunes or having healing remedies. This also suggests the role of millenarian religious movements that form a contrary position relative, especially in modernity, to a culture oriented primarily to advancement and security. Turner even suggests that in American culture the role of the Beat generation or of Hippies is to provide a form of living marked by spontaneity, immediacy, religious feelings, and a sharp sense of difference from settled or imposed social patterns. In some societies, the structured/liminal distinction takes the form of gender or ethnic distinctions and the obscuring or disregarding of such distinctions. In religious cultures, the recurring or ongoing representatives of the liminal are the Shaman or Prophet.

Departures from or exceptions to the reigning culture break through the interstices of structures as liminality, appear at the edges of structures as marginality, and arise from beneath structures as force. While in traditional societies both structure and potential are valued, Turner implies that potential, because a return to it is required, is more important. Order needs disruption, and difference needs commonality. Turner implies that early societies valued both sides of the dialectic, anti-structural as well as structural, but modern societies overvalue the structured and need, for their well-being, not to overlook or repress but to recognize and value exceptions to or freedom from structures.

Turner, therefore, turns attention to a stage exposed in and by rituals and to manifestations of that stage that hold the source of society's common life and its orderings. His argument or theory has continuing influence because of the meaning and role he associated with those people, groups, or movements not fully, if at all, integrated into a society, including those who often pursue radically different roles and goals from those that mark the established cultural and social situation. These people and expressions tend to be dismissed by established interests as alien, bizarre, or threatening, but, by relating them to the ritual processes of traditional societies, Turner gives them a role and value, even a primacy, that is striking. Again, we see in this an implied critique of modernity, which is marked by materiality, construction, and advance, a Romantic and religious retrieval of the roles of the marginalized, outcast, neglected, or repressed.

Conclusion

Although in many respects they differ from one another and have other, perhaps more central, concerns in their work than those noted, these five scholars reveal, whether intentionally or by cultural conditioning, a continuing and shared interest in their studies of religion. This shared interest focuses on a matter of importance for human life that tends in Western modernity to be neglected or repressed. Causing this neglect and repression is an increasing and eventually dominant cultural orientation toward advancement, power, and control, a cultural orientation that privileges the future at the expense of the past and present. Their studies of religion are drawn in varying degrees to the ways by which cultures, especially by their religions, recognize and even identify with matters located in the past or on the margins of awareness. What tends to be forgotten or overlooked by modern culture is recognized and affirmed in the religions of other or earlier cultures.

At the risk of oversimplifying, it is not off target to say that the orientation of modern Western culture toward the future is epitomized in and by a determining preoccupation with inventing, refining, and providing tools. To be a participant in modern culture, increasingly noticeable during the Victorian era, is to take for granted that the invention, improvement, and distribution of tools is an intrinsically valuable and shared interest because, among other things, it results in the reduction in people's lives of arduous, dangerous, and tedious labor and the increased understanding and amelioration of human illnesses and suffering. But more is included in this drive toward more and more effective tools. It is not only or so much that worthy goals are made approachable by tools, as that the development of tools grants those who possess them expanding knowledge and power. Newly invented means of producing tools made them more available to larger numbers of people and imparted to the culture a sense not only of increased security but also of superiority relative to those lacking the tools. An important and revealing line of development in modernity is the invention and deployment of the tools of warfare, the weapons of destruction, and eventually of mass destruction. It is important and revealing because it epitomizes the meaning and principal consequence of possessing and refining tools, namely, the acquisition and possession of power.

Three characteristics of a culture preoccupied with tools should be noted. The first is that it results not only in an orientation to the future but also in a reduction of interest in and regard for the past. A new or refined tool displaces its predecessors, and discontent with the tool that is presently available is an impetus to refine or replace it. While it may be interesting to remember how things were done before a certain tool for doing them was provided, few people would consider ignoring its replacement and retaining former ways of doing things. Outmoded and replaced tools become, at best, curiosities, and most often, waste and junk. Although the newest and most advanced tool is dependent upon earlier forms of it, those forms are displaced, cast aside, and forgotten.

The second characteristic of a culture preoccupied with tools is the growing prestige of power, a prestige granted not by worthy goals toward which power can be directed but granted by the possession of it. The power granted by tools can be used to further the interests of those possessing them at the expense of the interests of those who lack them. The acquisition and possession of power and control are not directed by shared and worthy goals but by the superiority they grant to those possessing them. This goal of superiority makes the quest for power compelling and even addictive because power elevates possessors of it above their environment, an environment that includes other people. Tools and the power they provide become less means toward worthy goals and more ends in themselves, particularly the goal of acquiring more power.

The third characteristic of a culture determined by a preoccupation with tools and means is that people are led by the culture to treat other people as tools or means, especially people with fewer tools and less power. When the acquisition and possession of power become a goal, other people or groups become competitors and obstacles because they are regarded as determined by the same goal. A zero-sum game arises by which power and the tools for or forms of it, especially financial wealth, are taken as worthy goals, and the more wealth one acquires, the more superiority relative to others one enjoys. Other people are seen, therefore, not first of all as persons but as competitors or threats. This attitude toward others is corrosive of culture. The goal of acquiring tools and the power they grant, especially wealth, leads to the treatment of people with less power as naturally deserving disregard or subjugation. This accounts in good part for the formation of class distinctions and their fixity in cultures. Certainly, all cultures are subject to social formations formed and fixed by inequalities of power, but in cultures other than high or late Western modernity there often can be found structures of meaning and value that are or can be shared by all participants and to some degree modify the use of power to form and maintain social distinctions. In Western modernity, many instances of these dynamics and their results can be found, particularly the subjugation of less powerful peoples. What comes under the heading of colonization and imperialism is, consequently, a major design in the fabric of Western advancement.

 A striking and revealing example of these dynamics is slavery and the role it plays in modernity. The capture, transport, sale, and ownership of Africans by the wealthy in Western countries, especially in the Americas, are not exceptional or odd in modernity, not aberrations. Slavery is an almost natural and inevitable consequence and culmination of a culture that leads to the treatment and use of other people as tools. Human beings are regarded not as persons but as means by which those in the quest for power, particularly in the form of wealth, use for gaining and retaining their social, economic, and political power. Slavery would still exist in the West if it were not for countering values and norms that gained enough presence to end it. But the results are still painfully evident in the continuing racism in modernity. Racism has many causes and supports, one of them being that slavery was built on treating people as tools that could be owned and used for the goal of increasing, retaining, and justifying the possession of power. When this ownership and use of people was outlawed, they could, like any other unusable tool, be cast aside. The descendants of slaves continued to be treated like tools that should be left behind, disregarded, or marginalized.

 Slavery and its continuing effects on the lives of Western people of African descent are obvious and continuing evidence of the dynamics of a culture defined primarily by the quest for power and the tools for gaining and deploying it, especially wealth. But it is not the only one. People, such as native Americans, are swept aside and marginalized. Because they are not usable, they lack value and, like peoples in colonized locations, are undeserving of the places they inhabit and can be removed from them. Examples such as these are not anomalies but central to an understanding of modernity and its faults and lacks.

 It would not be possible to cover all of the ways by which power, the quest for it and possession of it, reduces, fragments, and displaces culture, but two forms require mention while they are also too major and complex to be treated adequately here. One is the positions, roles, and experiences of women that in many, if not all, cultures have been determined by the power that males in the culture have gained and secured at the expense and use of women. One of the factors, a very important one, is the identification of women with functions, particularly sexual, procreative, and domestic. The reasons for and the defense of this reduction are too varied and complex to unfold here, but it is relevant to say, given the attention that this discussion has given to it, it is due, among many other factors, to the role of power in the definition of masculinity and the social, economic, and political means and justifications of identifying masculinity with the acquisition, retention, and uses of power. The second instance is the natural environment. It has also been functionally viewed and treated. Its value is determined by the uses that can be made of it or that it occasions or supports. Western modernity and the lack of respect and care for the environment cannot be separated, although there are also, now, as is also the case to some extent regarding the relation of women to power, increasingly noticeable and effective voices and movements designed to counter this disregard.

It is hoped that this brief and inadequate rehearsal of the faults in Western modernity created by a cultural orientation to power, advancement, and control is sufficient to take into account what this first orientation or shared aspect of the study of religion by the scholars treated in this chapter and to see its continuing relevance to cultural conditions in the present. However, it also calls attention to the fact that religion has not always played a critical and resistant role in relation to these negative cultural factors but has often contributed to their rise and continuation. More attention to this problem will be given in the second half of this book. Meanwhile, we can see that religious studies has among its major characteristics the critical exposure of the forces that cause and justify the neglect and repression not only of values but also of people because of its orientation to the future, to the acquisition and retention of power, and to the treatment of people as tools for or obstacles to furthering that design.

Chapter 3

STUDYING RELIGION AND THE LACK OF CULTURAL ACCESSES TO NEEDED INTANGIBLES

As we have seen, one interest in the development of religious studies has turned attention to aspects of life that are important and valuable but tend, by the orientation of modernity toward the future, toward invention, advancement, and control, to be neglected or repressed. These matters are primarily located as prior to, behind, below, or at the borders of more prominent preoccupations and are undervalued by them. We turn now to a second line of interests in the development of religious studies, one that also continues into our own time. This interest is in intangibles, particularly those related to personal identity and well-being, both individual and communal. Modern culture is seen as failing to provide access to them, and religion is seen as providing needed and lacking accesses. Studying other cultures and their religions exposes potentials in human life and relationships that are beneficial and needed but not readily accessible in modern culture. Studying other cultures and religions helps to identify what is lacking in current personal and relational life and indicates ways in which these lacks or needs can be addressed or redressed.

Herbert Spencer (1820–1903)[1]

Herbert Spencer is not an obvious selection as providing an example of religious studies shaped by attention to accesses to what people in their personal lives need but, due to the culture, lack. He was a civil engineer rather than a humanist, and his primary intellectual interests lay not so much in religion as in social institutions and how they establish and maintain themselves. Religion comes into his agenda primarily as a factor in the formation and

---

1 See especially Herbert Spencer, *The Principles of Sociology* (New York: D. Appleton & Company, 1897) Vol. I, "Ancestor Worship," pp. 285–328.

provision of social unity, particularly unity formed as a beneficial response to actual or potential threats. However, he deserves to be selected not only because of what he says about religion but also because he was widely read in Great Britain and the United States and, like James Frazer, was influential beyond academic circles.

Spencer's interest in and understanding of religion also deserves attention because he early on applied evolutionary theories to social and cultural history and carried them into the study of religion, thereby relating current interests in the idea of cultural progress to religion and modifying religion's reputation as opposing it. This also places his work in a position shared by scholars described in the previous chapter, namely, valuing and learning from earlier or other cultures despite developmental theories applied to cultural history.

It is important to note Spencer's strong interests in and high regard for social unity and his awareness that modern culture, due to the rapidity of mobility and increased complexity, reveals a need to address instabilities and to retain or reinstate identity, both personal and communal, as including continuity. This enabled him to cast religion in at least partially favorable light in terms of its help in providing stability and continuity for a culture undergoing rapid social and cultural change.

Spencer identifies threats, especially the threat of death, as a principal cause for the rise and formation of religious beliefs and practices. Death, a personal but socially shared threat, became related by religion to a realm that transcends human life, particularly a realm, it was believed, that those who died entered. In addition, societies that exchange nomadic for agrarian cultural patterns allow for burials, and burial sites become loci for religious rituals. By means of these rituals, the transcendent realm of the dead becomes less of a threat to the society's continuation and stability and more of a protector. As religions and societies advance, especially in and by their confidence in maintaining continuity and identity, a preoccupation with death decreases, although, since death retains its force despite social confidence, concern for the dead and awareness of the power of a transcendent realm persist. As religions evolve from simpler to more complex forms, they extend beyond an early preoccupation with death and the dead to additional threats to social life and identity.

What is powerful about Spencer's theory of the origins and persistence of religion in human life is that it finds grounding and validity in shared personal experiences. It can readily be acknowledged that members of a society, even if otherwise diverse, are unified in the face of threats they share. Threats to a people can produce not only cooperation between them but also feelings of mutuality within the group. It is not as though for Spencer religions arise solely because societies need the unity and stability that religions can provide. Religions also arise for other reasons, and one of them is that it not only addresses a shared awareness of death and other threats but also provides accesses to intangibles that persons and societies need, primarily personal and social identity. Fear and isolation are often responses to the negative realities that humans face, and people will readily identify with a group because such identification creates solidarity and eases the sense of vulnerability.

Since fear and isolation are expected human responses to adversities, it can be extended to include fear in the face of other, more immediate, threats both within and outside of society. The noticeable form this takes is fear of other societies and the need for political and military protection from and resistance to them. This allows political and military power to take on religious significance. This is also why the myths of traditional societies often deal with battles, celebrate heroes and victories, and associate political leaders and structures with transcendent approbation.

This emphasis of Spencer on the role of fear in the development of religion and on religion's role in the unification and stabilization of societies finds its contrary in his equally strong emphasis on personal individuality, even individualism. This side of him finds support in his social Darwinism. Indeed, "survival of the fittest" is initially his and not Darwin's phrase, and with it, he emphasizes a dynamic in societies that operates contrary to the need and desire within societies to be unified. This side of his work, this emphasis on the need of individuals to secure their personal status and roles, helped to make Spencer an influential theorist in nineteenth-century Britain and the United States. These contrary emphases in Spencer, the human need both for social inclusion and mutuality and for individual identity, were aspects of the culture in which Spencer was working, a culture that advanced unifying political and economic interests and, at the same time, celebrated individual heroes, such as political leaders, entrepreneurs, inventors, and artists.

While one could be turned away from Spencer because his theories seem to warrant preoccupation with individual and group survival, a trait of human life that, while it may be instinctive and biologically based, seems reductive, he also calls attention to the role of religion in granting meaning to social and personal identities. Religion is also operative in resisting the separation in societies of contrary relations between the need and desire for communal life and for individual advancement and well-being. While he did not finally resolve the tensions between such contraries, he clarified the need for both sides and implied that religion provides a way by which they can be held together. It is interesting to note that an older contemporary of Spencer who continues to be of interest to scholars, Alexis de Tocqueville, also identified the problem raised by the contrary attention to individual interests and social unity as especially acute for societies that exchange aristocratic or autocratic for more democratic forms of order.

While Spencer was an evolutionist in his understanding of religion, he did not predict religion's eventual demise as inevitable. Religion is a continuing factor in human life not only for the reasons already mentioned but also because concern for the unknown, the mysterious, and the threatening persists. Although advances in human knowledge and control reduce the scope of the mysterious and threatening, they will not dissolve them. Consequently, religion continues to play a role in both social and individual life. What needs constantly to be negotiated are not only such contraries as competition and cooperation, the individual and the corporate, or power and conciliation, but also the relations of the certain and the unknown, the mysterious and the controllable, fear and confidence. No matter how advanced and secured societies and individuals become, they will not be rid of uncertainty and vulnerability.

Among the contributions of Spencer to this second recurring or continuing interest or topic in religious studies, three seem to be particularly important. The first is a warning against exchanging the pervasive and recurring threats to well-being, such as natural threats to human life, for fear and negative views of other people. While the need and desire, both individual and social, for survival and security is ongoing, ontological threats should not be exchanged for social and political threats. Unfortunately, this exchange can easily be made, and threats to human life associated with hardship, loss, or death can be readily associated with other people both inside and outside of society.

A second contribution can be seen in the difference between Spencer's interests from those of theorists in the preceding chapter. The previous examples emphasized the human need for something vital and supportive that, by neglect or repression, is undervalued. Spencer, along with the other examples in this group, emphasizes basic and continuing human needs located in individual and relational personal life that continue in contemporary culture and that, at least to some degree, religion can address. Central among them is the commonality that can be felt not only in one's own group but more widely when recurring threats to personal and communal life or anticipations of them arise. Awareness of human life as shared is to be valued, and it deserves a place equal to individual interests and striving.

A third contribution is to grant religious beliefs and practices roots in human life that help to explain its persistence and value but also why it can be both a benefit and a bane to human well-being. Because cultures and religions can exchange a sense of threat from ontological or natural to social or political realities, it can have negative effects. We can infer that for Spencer religion needs and deserves understanding and even approbation but also critical attention and correction.

It is unfortunate that Spencer, because of his social Darwinism, is more often associated with such dominant characteristics of modernity as individual self-interest, the acquisition of power, and the advancement of some people at the expense of others than with clarifying the human need of something beneficial but widely lacking in modern culture, a need in relation to which religion's rise and role can be understood. He did not resolve all of the problems that his complex theory brings to attention, especially the relations between individual needs for identity and security and social unity and concerns, the relation of change and diversity to continuity and unity in cultural development, and the relations of ontological threats to the threats posed by other or alien social and political entities, but he implied that these persistent problems and the relation of religion to human life are intertwined with one another.

William James (1842–1910)[2]

There can be no hesitancy in putting forward the work of William James as exemplifying a recurring interest or topic in religious studies. Attention to his work continues, and it is an almost certain part of any introductory college course in religious studies. While his scholarly work is of continuing importance in several academic areas, I shall focus primarily on one of them, namely, the relevance of religion and the study of it to making accessible, especially to individuals, something intangible that is crucial to their personal life and well-being.

James was trained as a medical scientist and taught physiology and psychology at Harvard from 1886 on, where he established the first center for psychological research. In addition, he taught philosophy at Harvard, where he had as a colleague and philosophical contrary the absolute idealist Josiah Royce, and he helped to establish pragmatism as an American-based and widely disseminated philosophical position. His standing is bolstered by his family, especially his younger brother Henry, a major figure in the formation of the American literary tradition.

He addressed religion not in terms of early cultures and their development over time, as did most of the examples at which we are looking, but in terms of its place and role in the present. Even more important, he treated religion less in social and cultural terms and more as a matter of personal experience and feeling. Indeed, he gave academic standing to what continues today as a major

---

2 See especially William James, *The Varieties of Religious Experience: A Study in Human Nature* (London: Longmans, Green and Co., 1929), pp. 26–65.

religious concern in American culture, namely, the individual person, not so much now in what could, as with Spenser, be called material terms, such as striving to establish and maintain the bases for survival, but rather spiritual terms. His emphasis on the person also implied that religious institutions and authorities are secondary and dependent relative to individual religious experiences, an inversion he shares with early Romantic advocates of religion, such as the influential Christian theologian Friedrich Schleiermacher (1768–1834) and with the significant role in nineteenth-century American religious life of personal feelings and experiences.

James took as his primary data the experiences of exceptional, if also often eccentric, people. Ordinary religious people and religious institutions depend on these unusual sponsors. Since he locates the origins of religion in human exceptionalism, an interest also shared with the Romantics, and nonconforming individuality, he tends to emphasize less what religions have in common than their diversity—hence the use of the plural in the title of his Gifford Lectures and most well-known publication, *The Varieties of Religious Experience* (1902).

Religious experiences and feelings, as reported by visionaries and other originating persons, are not self-generated but are responses to something that comes to persons from without, a third matter of continuity with Romanticism, particularly the interest in the experience of the sublime. But James did not try to isolate religious experience from experiences of other kinds, such as fear, desire, joy, and guilt. What is for him particular in religious experiences is that they form an experiential compound occasioned by something that comes to a person and to which the person responds.

James gives a quite general, even vague, name to something that comes to a person in a religious experience. He calls it "more," and it is actualized in a person by way of the subconscious. The experience of "more," which evokes a cluster of feelings, should not be reduced to something other or less than it is, for example, to something neurological or sexual. He refers to such reductive interpretations of religious experiences as "medical materialism."

While James wanted to impart an inherent value to religious experiences, he also offered a way to evaluate them. As a pragmatist, his norm for evaluating religious experiences was not their roots or their absolutes but their fruits. Religious experiences should be valued not because they come by way of exceptional persons or because they may support religious doctrines or give rise to religious institutions so much as because they yield positive personal results—results that human beings need.

Primary among the fruits of religious experiences for James are experiences of the "more" that provide persons a way of feeling "at home" in the universe. In other words, the positive fruit of religious experience can be measured by its psychological benefits. For James, it is a healthy and even necessary thing for persons to feel positively related to something original, comprehensive, and enduring beyond themselves. Indeed, the well-being of persons is dependent upon a sense of relatedness to, enclosure within, or support from not so much social or cultural realities as the broader ontological context. This brings him to the assertion, one that he shares with other theorists in this chapter, that religion makes possible and accessible, either directly by means of experience or by participation made available in reports by others of religious experiences, what in any case is necessary for personal well-being, namely, a fundamental sense of being included and sustained by something intangible that lies outside or beyond a person to which a person feels positively related.

The process by which a person comes to feel at home in the universe takes two forms, depending on the kind of person who experiences it. There are for James, regarding religious experiences, two kinds of people. One kind is people who, naturally or by means of their nurture, already feel at home in the universe. These he calls "healthy-minded" people. While their feeling of being at home in the universe may vary in intensity or awareness, it is embedded within them. They take difficulties and disappointments in stride. The other kind is what he calls "sick souls." These are people who must undergo a change from a feeling of alienation or anxiety to feelings of acceptance and incorporation. They are people who need conversion. A reader of James would be justified in thinking that James is more interested in the second kind of person than in the first, in the process and consequence of an experience that brings a person from a sense of isolation and estrangement to a sense of inclusion is dramatic. And for James, this change or exchange, necessary and desirable for human well-being, is difficult to undergo apart from what he designates as religious experience. If it is true that James was particularly interested in persons who need to undergo a radical change in their relation to their world, it may be that, because of the increase of mobility in modern culture, people increasingly are displaced from their original settings and familiar supports and reside now in unfamiliar locations in which they do not feel at home.

Religious experiences and the changes they yield are so valuable for James that he is willing to put forward somewhat theological accounts of them. The "more" that is encountered in religious experiences is the divine, and it has several attributes. It is primary in the category of power and being; it evokes in the person feelings of solemnity and tenderness; and it generates in the person reverential attitudes toward it. The divine, then, is that which deserves persons' giving themselves over to it. By so doing, a person is granted a new sense of incorporation, participation, or affirmation that is crucial to personal well-being.

While James ventures into theology by his descriptions of the divine, he does not want to take conceptualizations of the divine literally. Such descriptions have an "as if" quality. He does not mean by this that descriptions of the divine are fictional or hypothetical; rather, they are approximate or metaphorical. They have this tentative or partial standing because what is experienced and what alters a person's location in the universe from alienation to feeling at home is something too comprehensive and primary adequately to be described. Indeed, the religious experience itself supports the attribution of an "as if" standing to descriptions of the divine because, in the religious experience, one has a sense of relatedness to something real that outstrips a person's understanding of it.

It becomes clear that, while James wants to emphasize the varieties of religious experience, he also recognizes continuity between them. For the sake of their well-being, all people need to feel "at home" in the world, and if they do not feel that way naturally or by virtue of their nurture, they must find it by other means. These other means are made available to people directly by religious experiences or indirectly by reports of such experiences provided by the people who have them. Also, religious experiences, while they are radical, do not separate people from their ordinary contexts. Experiences of the divine, while distinguishable from other experiences, are also continuous with the relations religious persons have with other realities.

For James, religion can generally be thought of as natural. While the divine is not the same thing as nature, it is related to the natural as being comprehensive and positive in its overall qualities and effects. One can feel at home in the universe because the universe is already, at least in good part or potentially, a person's home. In addition, the well-being of a person and what it is natural for a person to be, namely at home in the universe, are mutually supportive. Alienation and anxiety contribute to and are signs of stress and even mental illness. Religion grants access, then, to what in any case is needed, and the fruit of religion is its contribution to mental health and personal well-being.

Finally, James is addressing the nature of religious experiences in a cultural context in which mobility and a diminished sense of belonging are increasing and, for many people, radical and unremitting. The increasingly pervasive and determining contexts of modern life are not natural or familiar but, especially in large urban contexts, impersonal, massive, material, powerful, and external. The study of religious experiences gives access for James and his many readers to something needed and available, namely, an exchange of isolation and alienation for a feeling of reassuring and meaningful incorporation. Without religion the lack in modernity of access to ways by which people can be incorporated by a reality that is more or other than what is humanly made and controlled will likely go unaddressed.

Emile Durkheim (1858–1917)[3]

Emile Durkheim's *The Elementary Forms of Religious Life*, which was published in 1916, is a classic both for the advance of sociology as one of the human sciences and for the rise of religious studies. It directs attention to the social roles and functions of religion that Durkheim took as not simply an aspect or byproduct of religion but as central to it. He emphasized the community-granting function of religion, and he may have been drawn to this function because he was himself Jewish and was working in a Catholic culture. For both of these traditions, the communal identity granted by religion and its rituals are major factors.

As a social scientist, Durkheim did not base his understanding and study of religion on something ontological, transcendent, or deeply buried in persons. Nor did he treat religion as arising from something that could be explained in nonreligious terms. His approach, by implying the important role of religion in human life, also preserved the integrity and significance of the subject. He pointed to a need in personal and relational life that, if not addressed by religion, should somehow in any case be met.

While Durkheim was attentive to forms of religious life in his own day, he emphasized what was elementary in early forms because he thought that they were more clearly detectable. And he saw the elementary or early forms of religious life as continuing into the present, as defining the characteristics of religion, and as constituting what religions have in common.

Durkheim posits as central to religion something that most everyone has experienced as powerful and exhilarating, namely, being caught up in the spirit of a group event. Whether the group-feeling comes from singing in a choir, marching in a parade, participating in a demonstration, or cheering for a sports team, the individual person is caught up by a shared feeling or spirit, and the experience can be intense and memorable. Durkheim contends that this group-feeling is not simply the sum of contributions that individuals make to an event but is something more, even unique, something particular to the group and the occasion itself. Finally, he contends that people not only desire events and experiences of this kind and benefit from them when they occur but also need them. In a study of suicide rates in various social units, he concluded that suicidal frequency was greater among Protestants than among Catholics and Jews, suggesting that this was due to the greater emphasis in the latter traditions on group identity and participation. He implies that group identity is basic to personal well-being.

---

3 See especially Emile Durkheim, *The Elementary Forms of Religious Life*, trans. Joseph Ward Swain (Glencoe, IL: Free Press, 1947), pp. 1–47.

What is true for more specific groups and communities is true as well for societies more generally. A society needs not only structure and regulation; it also needs a spirit of commonality, one that gives individuals a sense of participation in something that is shared, something to which they can contribute, and something that is greater and even more important than they are themselves. The need for inclusion and a shared identity is especially granted by religion. Other aspects of religion, such as beliefs and practices, have their importance by contributing to the central aspect of religion, the sense of inclusion in and by a group or community. A basic human need and the role of religion can, then, converge.

While he relates the sense of inclusion that religion can provide with group-feelings or experiences that more widely and generally occur, he also sees religious experiences of inclusion as distinguishable from other forms. This is due primarily to the distinction that religion provides between the sacred and the profane. This is a distinction more basic than that between good and evil, natural and supernatural, or material and spiritual. The sacred and the profane are distinguishable from and contrary to one another. Religion's orientation is toward the sacred and away from the profane. The sacred itself, however, is not hidden or internal; it is external and shared. An elementary representation of the sacred is the totem, a visible object that epitomizes or evokes the shared identity and spirit of the group, its values, aspirations, and destiny. The totem, then, is an external representation of the essence of the group. To identify with the totem is to identify with the group. While "totem" refers to a specific kind of sacred object, the term can also be used more broadly to include any object that a group recognizes as expressive of its spirit and identity. A flag, a monument, or the picture of a leader can function as a totem, and a person's attention to it is a form of that person's recognition of and identification with not only the object but also the communal spirit it inspires and represents.

For Durkheim, rituals and rites are actions that turn attention to the power and significance of the sacred and extend that power and significance into the life of the group and thereby also to its individual participants. They relate participants not only to the sacred but also to one another as a group and the group to the larger world. Rituals and rites give to members of a group or society a sense of continuity between their own identity and their larger communal and social contexts. It should be noted again that rites and rituals are particularly recognizable features of Jewish and Catholic religious life.

As with the other examples considered in this chapter, religion is important for Durkheim because it provides real and sacred intangibles that, in any case, are necessary, primarily the identity granted to persons by their inclusion in a group or society that is larger, more enduring, and more significant than they are themselves. If religion does not provide this experience, it must be provided in some other way. This is why there often are religious qualities in political and other ceremonies and occasions, even though their explicit purpose may not be religious. There is for Durkheim a relation between the sacred in religious life and the kind of exhilaration people feel when they get caught up in a group spirit. It can be assumed that everyone knows what such an experience is like and can recall occasions when it occurred. Indeed, it seems that for Durkheim, exhilarating and inclusive occasions of group-feeling, the need for and provision of them, are, while related and even indebted to religion, deeper and of a greater extent than religion itself.

Questions can arise concerning Durkheim's largely positive treatment of group-feeling or identity. For him, the contrary or negative alternative to it is isolation and the loss of identity or self-worth, and group identification can counter these negatives. But group feeling and identification can also be, as we saw in Spenser, generated not only by the exclusion of others or outsiders but also by hostility toward other groups. Group behaviors also reveal that individuals as parts of a group are enabled to engage in more destructive and cruel acts than when they act as individuals. One thinks, to indicate only a single example, of mob violence that occasionally follows sporting events.

While questions may arise, no doubt can be raised about what, in studying religion, Durkheim considers of central interest. His emphasis on the group or on society counters the stress on individuality that affects many understandings of religion, due, perhaps, to the widespread influence in American religion and religious studies of Protestantism. Also, Durkheim provides a counterweight to the focus in Western theories on the identity of individual persons, since identity is not only personal and internal but also external and communal in its source and force. Also, Durkheim calls attention to something that is unusual and very effective while also being generally accessible and understandable. The feeling of being included in and by a group, along with its contrary, namely, being excluded or alienated, are powerful and significant experiences that, while being immediately recognizable and universally shared, are also powerful, meaningful, and distinct. Durkheim's theory also allows us to see why religion is so deeply embedded in the lives of people and so important for them. Finally, his theory, while it may raise questions by its designation of something general as something that includes religion, helps to explain why people who can be called or consider themselves to be nonreligious participate in rituals and rites that have, by virtue of their cultural or social importance, solemnity, and a potential to inspire enthusiasm and other religion-like effects.

Max Weber (1864–1920)[4]

Max Weber's interests in religion have a noticeable academic role and standing because he combined attention to religion with many other interests, historical, social, and economic. He also gave religion, among these interests, a role in the daily lives of people because for him religion gives people an intangible that in any case they need, namely, a sense of a meaningful role or purpose in the world. Religion motivates people, gives them goals and values to which they aspire, and grants significance to their lives and activities. Since he emphasized religion as giving people an understanding of how to act in and relate to their world, his emphasis was as much on religious beliefs as on religious practices or feelings. An important point to be made, relative to his place in this chapter, is the implication left by his work that the motivations and purposes provided to people by their religion are not optional but need to be in place so that without religion this important personal, social, and even economic sense of role and purpose becomes a question in need of an answer.

Weber is well-known for his book on the relation between Protestant Christianity and the rise of capitalism in the modern West. He argued, in *The Protestant Ethic and the Spirit of Capitalism* (1905) that Protestant Christianity took traditional religious attitudes and values out of the monastery and applied them to daily living. This imparted a religious significance to daily life and ordinary work. Work became, then, more of a calling than a mundane necessity; it also provided a sense of personal value and social contribution. Protestantism also stressed frugality and postponement of gratification, and these attitudes supported capitalism as well. His case for religious factors as causal for the rise of capitalism is striking because it delivered economic life from wholly material accounts, such as those related to the acquisition of power and the drive for survival.

Consistent with his stress on individual motivation and industry, Weber also emphasized the religious roles of charismatic leaders as having motivational and meaning-granting effects on people. The powerfully energizing and directing effect of leaders on large numbers of people is due to the source of charismatic influence being more than personal. Weber gave attention to the roles in religion played by leaders and the more than individual power ascribed to leaders by the people they influence. Belief in something that transcends human agency spreads or deepens into belief in spiritual reality, and this helps to explain why religion becomes not only a motivational and directional means but also an end in itself.

---

4 See especially Max Weber, *The Protestant Ethic and the Spirit of Capitalism*, trans. Talcott Parsons (London and New York: Routledge, 1993), pp. 47–92.

Weber's theory continues to have force in academic circles because, among other reasons, it has an empirical base. Religion provides an answer to an otherwise observed phenomenon to which no other answers seem to have equal adequacy or plausibility: What gives people a sense of purpose, of their daily lives and work as having meaning? While his answer to the question is simple, namely, that religion does this, the answer also allows for relating religious and cultural factors to personal and group identities.

Societies and their religions should be understood, then, as deserving an appreciative understanding that Weber calls *Verstehen*. Understanding people means taking into account not only their material interests and contexts but also their moral and religious beliefs, what motivates and directs their actions and relates them to their ordinary lives and to one another. Leaders, while they share characteristics that grant to them the power to motivate and direct people, differ from one another as to the kinds of beliefs and goals that their influence produces. This theory of religion as arising from the effects produced in people by the influence of leaders continues to occupy a place in religious studies and to give rise to interests in spiritual leaders and their inspiring and motivational influences.

In addition to the fact that his theories combine both generally applicable elements and recognition of differences and particularities, Weber continues to be important because, like other examples in this chapter in their differing ways, he saw religion as providing people something intangible that they need for their well-being and sense of personal value. This was for him not so much giving people a sense of being at home in the universe, as with James, or of being included in a meaningful group, as with Durkheim, as giving people the assurance that their activities, aspirations, and goals carry inherent meaning and value. Furthermore, Weber's theories combine individual, social, cultural, and economic interests. Personal life and the broader social and economic context can and, to some degree, do relate to one another. Put another way, it can be said that Weber's understanding of Protestant culture's profound influence on the rise of capitalism epitomizes his theory, since it creates and warrants both personal and social formations and establishes their mutuality.

Weber's theory, while it distinguishes the spiritual or transcendent from the mundane, does not separate the two from one another. Religion, as it develops, becomes an area of life that has its own important role, but neither the spiritual realm nor a religion is separated by him from ordinary life. The study of religion, then, does not abstract religion. Religion can be recognized not only as something private and separate but also as permeating the lives of ordinary persons and affecting social formations and participation.

Weber's theory also introduces questions that it seems unable adequately to answer. One of them arises from his theory of kinds of authority, which he tends to arrange chronologically. In addition to charismatic, there also are traditional and bureaucratic forms of authority. These have the results, among other things, of giving less importance to individual motivation and more to order. Traditional forms of authority, epitomized by the passing down of positions in royal lineages, designate less the gifts of the leader and more the office, even though in some ancient societies designated leaders had to validate their positions by success in battle or in breeding heirs. Bureaucratic authority has an even clearer contrary relation to individual spontaneity and agency. This form of authority, fashioned by more rationalistic cultures, establishes a structure into which persons are expected to fit and to which they are expected to conform. Since the bureaucratic structure is deemed to be rational and efficient, attempts to change it, lest they appear to be irrational or inefficient, must be turned toward making the structure more rational and efficient, that is, more bureaucratic. Because bureaucratic forms of authority and their consequent social, economic, and political structures are typical outcomes of modernity and of the importance of rationality and efficiency in and for it, the continuing role of religion, with its relation to the influence of charismatic leaders and personal motivation and aspiration, becomes questionable. While people complain and even joke about the bureaucratic control of their lives, it is not clear what the role of religion in modern societies can be, according to Weber. However, while Weber does not seem to resolve the tension between the roles of religion in personal lives and the effects of modern bureaucracies on them, his theory accounts for the sense of unease or alienation that is a prominent part of modern culture due to a lack of access to personal and group sources of meaningful motivations and goals.

Weber seems to leave us, then, with both an assessment of the human need for beliefs and norms that motivate people to act in relation to worthy goals and of the role of religion in providing those beliefs and, in contrast, an assessment of modernity primarily determined by a rationality that structures public life and requires people to conform to that structure. As a scientist, Weber is dedicated more to description and analysis than to evaluation, and this may account for the lack of resolution to the questions his theories and analyses pose. But it seems that the major role he assigns to religion as providing people with motivation and goals imputes a high value to it. It follows that modernity, with bureaucracy as its dominant form of authority, is in tension with the roles and consequences of religion as he describes them. This raises a question as to how Western modernity, in its relation to the human need for meaningful roles and goals, is to be evaluated. The answer seems to be negative. If so, we have here an appraisal of the relation of religion to modern Western culture that posits not an outmoded role for religion relative to the lacks in the culture but, rather, the problem created for a society by a form of authority that fails to support, as religion once did, the human need for meaningful purpose in daily life generally and in work or vocation particularly.

Robert Bellah (1927–2013)[5]

A fifth example of scholars whose studies of religion draw attention to intangibles important to human well-being and made accessible by religion is Robert Bellah. Known for his remarkable erudition, Bellah was educated at Harvard University, receiving his doctoral degree with a dissertation on the sociology of Japanese religion. He spent two years in Montreal studying Islam, returned to Harvard to teach there for ten years, and then moved to the University of California at Berkeley, where he spent the rest of his career.

Bellah combined many areas of scholarship, and his reach was very wide. His knowledge allowed him not only to comment on various religious traditions but also to argue that the religious behaviors of human beings find their roots in the behaviors of animal species. While tracing human back to pre-human behaviors and societies, he provided a natural grounding for what he emphasized as important for human well-being and made accessible, although not exclusively, in religion. His interests stretched from early life to modern culture, including analyses of contemporary American society.

A principal point drawn from his study of animal behaviors is that animals take time off from the necessities governing their lives and turn to play. This time apart is clearly recognizable. There may be tussle and even struggle during playtime, but there is no finality or harm done. Animals learn this from early days when they are toyed with by their parents or siblings. Bellah also takes as crucial the emergence of lactation, the calm, warm, and comforting intimacy offered by maternal care. Not only are these moments in animal life distinguishable from everyday behaviors; they also have an ethical status. The rules of play establish the distinction between what is permissible and what is out of bounds, and maternal care is not only a necessity but also a good, a gift.

These interests in the relations of human to animal life do not mean that Bellah was sentimentally attracted to early life and resistant to progress. He is also known for his theory of the stages of religious development in human societies. There are five of them, and they indicate a line of progress toward greater differentiation, comprehension, and rationality.

---

5 See especially Robert N. Bellah, *Religion in Human Evolution* (Cambridge, MA: Harvard University Press, 2011), pp. 1–43.

The first is Primitive and is oriented by a single cosmos, one that assumes continuity between the mythical and the actual. Virtually every mountain, rock, or tree is related to the actions of mythical beings, and human actions have their mythical prototypes. The mixture of mythical and actual is also present in ritual. Primitive religions lack priests, and organization within them is fluid.

The second stage is Archaic. Here, a distinguishable culture arises with particularized gods, priests, and rituals. Myth and ritual are systematized or elaborated, and mythical beings are more specifically characterized.

The third stage is Historic, and its principal feature is a turn toward the authority or power of the transcendent as a primary and meaningful realm. The religious goal is deliverance from the mundane into relation to the transcendent. Accordingly, the mundane and humans themselves are deficient or flawed. While the authority of the transcendent can serve to enforce religious establishments, it also, and perhaps primarily, increases the chances for particularity and even disestablishment.

The fourth stage is Early Modern religion, which Bellah finds most clearly recognizable in Protestant Christianity. What the Reformers did was to circumvent the structure of religious mediation and authority and to recognize the ordinary person as having the potential for a more direct relation to the transcendent. In ways resembling Weber's theory, the whole of life becomes an arena for religious actions, and the quality or direction of personal life, the life of faith, becomes normative.

The final stage, which marks contemporary religion in the West, places responsibility for religious life in and with persons who are expected to clarify for themselves what, if anything, religion shall be or mean. This is accompanied by a decline of conformity in religious life to institutional, doctrinal, or behavioral traditions and norms. The religious institution, if it plays a part at all, does so by providing an environment in which people can find encouragement and some directives for pursuing what the other members of the institution, in their own ways, are also engaged by. It is assumed that the resources for establishing one's religious identity are not confined to particular texts, institutions, or practices but can also be found in other religions and in secular art and thought.

A third thing for which Bellah is well known is his emphasis on what he once called Civil Religion. Drawing particularly on Durkheim, Bellah attends to religion not only in relation to individual persons but also to its social roles. For him human well-being is not solely an individual pursuit but is also bound to responsibilities for the common good. Americans live with a tension between what he sometimes calls the "Republican" side, which has an ethical, educational, and even spiritual role regarding citizenship, and a liberal side, which encourages the free pursuit of self-interests. For Bellah, emphases during the twentieth century increasingly shifted away from a balance and toward self-interest epitomized for him by the importance, particularly in university life, of a Rational Choice theory of values, a theory that makes self-interest primary. Bellah makes the case for the "Republican" side by relating it to what he called "habits," that is, acquired and embedded concerns, particularly for the well-being of others. Another form he gives to this tension is the distinction between knowledge as information, along with the power it gives, and knowledge as meaning, the sense we have of the significance of the larger world and of our place in it.

In his extensive study of 2011, *Religion in Human Evolution*, Bellah posits a distinction in social and personal life between the realm of necessary daily activities and a realm of freer activities, such as watching a movie or a sporting event. His point is that people need the second of these two realms because they cannot stand to live in the ordinary world all the time. Indeed, the point is even more strongly made: art, sports, vacations, and other times and places apart challenge the assumption that the realm of daily responsibilities and activities is the more real and important one. This is because the realm apart is oriented not by 'deficiency' cognition, which drives us toward practical actions, but by 'being' cognition, which grants participants a sense of inclusion and wholeness that transcends particularity. The implication is clear and carries some similarities to the interests of other figures in this chapter: the realm of the ordinary and practical not only creates the need for the realm of inclusion and wholeness but is less important and dependent on it. Without the opportunity for what could be called the transcendence that 'being' cognition offers, the everyday becomes a prison or deadening grind. What for Bellah is optimal is that these two realms, which find their roots or counterparts in animal societies, rather than separated from one another be in some degree related so that one's daily activities and work are supported by the meaning and wholeness-granting realm of 'being' cognition.

When he turns attention to contemporary Western societies, Bellah contends that this gratuitous realm of human inclusion does not receive the kind of recognition it deserves. Everything, including the arts and sports, has been affected and even usurped by the realm of competition, success, and cost/benefit value assessments. Like Durkheim, he insists that personal identity is not only individual but is also social, and it involves, in addition to individual interests, the well-being of the community. The twentieth century, he argues, has seen a shift in American society away from social responsibility and toward self-interest. Concern for others and motivations based on ideals concerning the greater good should be retrieved and re-embedded in the moral fiber of people. Religion can help to do this. Religion provides access to a realm of 'being' cognition and grants to that realm its necessary status as primary relative to the realm of 'deficiency' cognition. Its qualities of inclusion and renewal, while neglected by the realm of 'deficiency' cognition and the business of providing for daily needs, grant persons access to a transcendence, inclusion, and sense of wholeness without which the obligations and needs of ordinary life become isolating and oppressive.

For Bellah the realm that stands as an alternative to the ordinary is not an abstraction or ideal; he views it in his work empirically. He argues that our society jeopardizes its future when it ignores that to which religions grant access, namely, a realm related to but separable from the ordinary and mundane in which "habits of the heart" can be formed and nurtured. Without at least something of what religion offers and has offered in the past, other means, such as art, sports, vacations, and social gatherings, will tend to take on the characteristics of the ordinary world, that is, the world of self-interest, competition, and power. Religious Studies can remind us of the perdurable status of a realm that not only can redeem us, if only temporarily, from the effects on us of daily responsibilities but can also release us back into the ordinary to affect it, at least to some degree, by attitudes acquired and reinforced by what is non-ordinary and gracious. The ordinary is, to use his term, deficient, and it not only needs the realm of being as an alternative to it but also needs it if it is not itself to become untenable. Religion and the study of it can make us aware of access to intangibles that are needed by persons and society but are threatened by the expanding realm of deficiency, namely, an alternative realm of inclusion, restoration, and meaning.

Conclusion

The five examples considered in this chapter, however much they differ from one another, turn attention to the accesses religion provides to intangibles that are needed for human well-being. Implied is the point that modernity does not readily enough provide such accesses and, indeed, if left to itself drains personal and corporate life of its identity, meaning, and purpose. If one would want a summarizing concern in these critiques of modernity, it would be their awareness that within modern culture personal alienation and loneliness aggravated by feelings of vulnerability and meaninglessness are prominent and even defining. A shared interest in their studies counters such negative states by the access religion provides to positive, corrective, and intangible potentials, especially those granting a sense of inclusion, purpose, and meaning. While they vary in their answers to the question of whether what is needed can also be addressed outside of religion, they agree that there is something about religion and, by extension, the study of religion that brings to the fore awareness of needs in modern culture that must be met in order to increase personal and social well-being. They also imply that modern culture has a pervasiveness and force that makes these needs intensely felt and that religion should be understood, if not appreciated, as responding to these lacks by providing people access to intangible realities that in any case they need.

The shared interest in religious studies found in these examples, namely, accesses to intangibles that ameliorate human deficiencies and needs, seems obviously and increasingly relevant to current cultural conditions. One way of approaching this situation is by taking up the question of personal identity. In a culture determined by massive and impersonal materialist structures and dynamics, many of them imposed as necessities on the culture, especially in and by urban living, the question of who one is becomes a matter not only uprooted from supportive and nurturing contexts but also impacted by contexts that have little regard or support for personal identity and integrity. The question is how one can be a person when the dominant culture does not provide adequate resources and occasions for intangible experiences and leaves the question of personal identity to improvised resolution.

While differing from one another in their answers to this question, the five examples agree that being a person is not a matter only or even primarily of material position or wealth but also of relation to something outside the individual and material that is as, if not more, important than the person. Implied by this relation or orientation to something of value or significance outside oneself is that it has its importance to some degree by bringing to persons resources other or more than their own. That to which a person is invited to relate is not simply a continuation or confirmation of self-interest. This something more is, while recognizable and accessible, something other. This means that, to some degree, personal identity and integrity are not so much gained as they are received as gifts given in and by relationships or incorporation.

Religious studies, in its continuing attention to this second interest, can infer from the examples offered that at least three characteristics of late modern culture aggravate the lack that religion is presented here as addressing. The first is the widespread and deeply embedded assumption that identity, whether of a person or of a group, is secured oppositionally. "I am" and "we are" are established or at least clarified by not being like others. Difference defines. Some of this is unavoidable, even, perhaps, natural. Maturation is a process of distinguishing oneself to some noticeable degree from others, including one's parents and siblings. This distinguishing can easily involve competitiveness: "I can do what that person does or I can be what that person is, but I can do it or be it better." This form of distinguishing oneself from others is not necessarily objectionable, although it often creates a self-identity not only by difference but also by opposition and superiority. However, competition is also a pathway to improvement and advancement, both personal and cultural. One admires, imitates, and outdoes others, and this is how improvements and advances arise. What is crucial in this process of achievement, however, is what a person or group sees as a goal, and that goal rather than the sense of success or superiority in achieving it evokes and warrants the effort. Opposition and competitive forms of self-actualization and identity are, to a degree, natural and necessary, but they should defer to the "more" outside oneself that is affirmed by a person's or group's regard for it and inclusion by it.

What needs to be added is that the significance and value of that which stands outside a person and a group and to which they need to defer is intangible or non-material. This means that accessing it requires belief. Surely, reasons can be given to validate something intangible that is chosen by a person or group as a goal and aspiration. And something is lacking if a person or group is oriented to and by an object or goal obviously unworthy of the devotion or effort directed to it. But accessing or receiving the intangible requires a belief that is not reducible to the reasons that may be given in an explanation or defense of it. These beliefs need not be religious; many people are dedicated to causes, organizations, other people, or goals and aspirations that warrant their regard but are not religious. But religion necessarily carries within it the occasions, practices, and beliefs that direct the attention of devotees to something outside themselves that has meaning and value warranting the formation of identity in relation to it.

A major complication for the study of religion that posits this second interest as of continuing importance is that religion itself so often promotes identities, whether personal or group, that depend on or result in distinction from, disregard for, opposition to, and superiority over other people. Religious studies, as we shall more fully see in the second part of this guide, should, in the face of these conditions, make clear the internal guards provided by religion for attributing the value or importance of that to which a person or group aspires not to what lies outside or beyond them but to the person or group themselves.

Another major cultural factor that affects attention to and raises questions for this second interest in religious studies, namely, access to intangibles that people need, is the widespread and increasing importance of relating personal identity to an intangible called "spirituality." People find it increasingly possible to self-identify neither as religious nor as nonreligious but as spiritual, which opens a large middle ground between the clearer alternatives of religious and nonreligious. This middle ground is generally not specific but constitutes a kind of potential to which persons and, at times also groups, can give a particular shape. Vagueness is increased when spirituality is characterized as a "journey" that one undertakes in life, and this trope secures not an existent or shared path toward personal actualization but a personally charted process. Our five examples, while also somewhat uncertain concerning the intangible to which they direct attention, present it as a recognizable and shared human experience.

Recounting the presence of spirituality in religious traditions within the modern period and traditions, especially East Asian, that have become more common to Western culture, would take us away from this book's agenda. However, it is important to say that the various forms of spirituality within established religious traditions or for the formation of more recent religious identities and communities have become a part of the present scene. This turn was and continues to be a reaction to the increasing effects of materialism on the culture and on personal and group identities, a reaction noticeably initiated in and by Romanticism. It is marked by increased and more intentional interest in personal and internal life, including feelings, imagination, and beliefs. The value of renewed attention to internal human experiences cannot be gainsaid. It is natural and warranted, in the face of massive, impersonal, and controlling material conditions, to raise awareness of the importance of personal particularity, identity, and integrity. However, this turn also requires discrimination between a beneficial regard for personal identity and integrity and a kind of self-preoccupation often suggestive of narcissism. It can lead as well to a neglect of one's dependence on and responsibilities for corporate life. Again, this raises questions and problems for religious studies because, while people can insist on their being spiritual without being religious, there is no doubt that this position may be based on attributing to the self not only particularity but also self-preoccupation. This turn or result is opposed by the examples at which we have looked because these examples emphasize the potential in religion for personal formation accessed by intangible realities that are outside and more than oneself and can also be shared.

A third culturally recognizable current complicating this second line of interest in religious studies, is the tendency to think of personal identity as a possession. Identity readily becomes something a person acquires, forms, and, in a word, owns. Personal identity becomes less who or what one is and more who or what one has. It is interesting and perhaps illuminating to see a corresponding use of possessive language for the relation of people to time and temporality. Time is often referred to as something one possesses, has, spends, saves, wastes, or uses. But time is basically or primarily given. We are born in a time that is granted to us and is, at the end, taken away. Something similar can be said of personal identity. It is basically or primarily given to us and becomes a possession only secondarily and tentatively.

Personal identity as possession readily relates identity to acquisition. When identity is primarily a possession, what one acquires and possesses not only relates to but also confirms who one is. And what one most obviously possesses is not intangible but material. The principal result of tangible possessions is to grant power, and a major form of power is economic, is wealth. A major agenda item for religious studies is to address questions related to the thirst and quest for wealth. These questions are complicated by the fact that religious studies are carried out in institutions, the viability of which depends on wealth, either generated by or contributed to them. This dependence has also turned the structure and content of higher education increasingly toward financial, that is, material, concerns. Institutions of higher education have themselves increasingly assumed the shape and behavior of businesses, with administrators as managers, faculty as employees, and students as customers. Curricula are determined by customer demand, and students have increasingly been determined in their studies by the financial opportunities to which their academic achievements will lead. The question becomes whether or not religious studies with this second interest revealed by these examples can position itself clearly in a contrary relation not only to the culture more generally but to academic culture as well. Can religious studies help to make the case that crucial to human well-being is access to intangibles that relate persons and groups to something that is other and more than one's self? Can religious studies, if it pursues this second interest, find traction on a terrain determined by personal identity as a matter of self-preoccupation and the acquisition of wealth?

Chapter 4

STUDYING RELIGION AND THE CULTURAL NEED FOR MORE ADEQUATE WORLDVIEWS

We turn now to a third interest in religious studies that is shared over a stretch of time and continues to be important. It is the relation of religion to the human need for an adequate worldview. For the scholars treated in this chapter, adequate or workable worldviews were or are granted to people by their culture and religion, but modernity has caused or witnessed the breakdown of such provisions. This is due largely to modern culture having been divided into separate and largely unrelated parts. These separated parts are shaped by contrary orientations, religious and secular, internal and external, moral, spiritual, or meaningful and material. While some people live and understand their worlds by their orientation primarily or exclusively to one or the other of these two sides, people who relate to both realms find it increasingly difficult to bring or hold them together. Religion is relevant to this situation because in the past, in other cultures, and for some people, religion helps to relate both sides to one another. The question is how, if at all, religion can be seen to have potentials for recognizing within the larger and nonreligious realm concerns to which it can relate or lacks which it can address. Can religion still contribute to the formation of a shared, workable, and unified worldview, or has it been deprived of that role?

A major factor contributing to the separation of personal and public interests from one another is the increasing gap between scientific and technological advancements, accounts of the world, and goals, on the one hand, and worldviews provided by inherited cultural and religious beliefs and principles, on the other, a gap that became culturally visible in the mid-nineteenth century. A major moment in the cultural disestablishment of religion in modern academic and public life can be marked by the 1859 publication of Darwin's discoveries and theories and in 1860 by the publication in the English-speaking world of implications for biblical authority created primarily by German historical and textual scholarship. These two publications called wide attention to the growing division in the culture between differing if not contrary accounts of nature and history, of religiously and nonreligiously sponsored worldviews. The tension and even conflict between traditional or religious views and views increasingly pervasive and determining, continue into the present day and have become an almost central characteristic of late modernity. A complex question arises for religious studies, then, as to whether or not the provision of a unifying and workable worldview continues to be a human need and whether or not religion can be recognized as a constitutive part of it. The question arises in a context in which present conditions and their dynamics seem more to resist than to encourage raising this question and, even more, to answering it by giving religion a contributing role in forming a more adequate worldview.

The separation into two differing if not contrary cultural realms can be seen as arising in modernity before the more religiously occasioned separation occurred in the nineteenth century. This earlier separation is related to Romanticism. The increasingly determining effects of industrialization and urban life and their rapid expansion, the wresting of people's lives from their rooted communities into locations that had no clear regard for personal histories or communal values, and the relation of particular communities to the larger world by means of more rapid and extensive modes of transportation and communication caused changes and complexities that were increasingly difficult to house culturally and to include in a shared worldview. Romanticism, therefore, set the stage for the visible division between religion and intellectual, especially scientific and technological, interests. These cultural conditions and dynamics persist, perhaps in even more aggravated forms, into the present day. It is relevant to these conditions to recognize a degree of mutuality between religion and aspects of Romanticism in both having locations as exceptions or resistances to the increasingly dominant features and forces of modernity, particularly materialism.

A major effect of a divided culture such as this is to separate personal needs, potentials, and relations from social and economic conditions, feelings and values from external dynamics, and meaning and morality from material. Modernity, epitomized by science and technology, supported and even advanced, if only implicitly, a social, economic, and political account of the world increasingly recognizable as materialist. But materialism, which tends not only away from the personal and toward the determined, has little in it to account for the role of human values, responsibilities, and creativity. This inadequacy produces divisions and tensions not only between religious and nonreligious and between personal and public interests but also between idealist or spiritual and materialist accounts of human beings, their world, and their relations to and within it.

Religious studies emerged, then, in the context of an increasingly felt lack of a coherent and shared account of the lived world that would reduce the separations from and tensions between one another of these two major components of an adequate and shared worldview. A line of formative work in religious studies can be seen as addressing this lack of coherent and shared worldviews and as raising the question of whether religion, at least in part, is relevant to this lack. Can an adequate worldview be retained or framed that would bring or hold together the material and the spiritual, the personal and the public, and the internal and the external? We shall look now at five examples of researchers and theorists of religion who, to varying degrees and in various ways, address this third major interest in and for religious studies, namely, religion's role in or contribution to an inclusive, workable, and shared worldview.

Edward B. Tylor (1832–1917)[1]

E. B. Tylor is noteworthy, among other things, for holding the first chair in the field of anthropology at Oxford University from 1896 to 1909. He formulated his theories of religion in close relation to his anthropological studies, particularly in Mexico and among the Australian Aborigines. One of his more important conclusions is that religion is not an occasional or secondary development in the rise of human cultures but always and everywhere present in and basic for them. Human cultural development and religion are mutually implicated. This observation, among other things, counters the assumption that the two factors, cultural advancement and religion, are fundamentally and necessarily contrary to one another. Another of his conclusions is that religion plays, even in early cultures, a detectable philosophical role. Religion in early cultures provides principles for constructing an account of why things are the way they are and happen as they do.

Perhaps because of his Quaker background, Tylor saw religion not primarily as a social but as a personal matter, that is, the sense people have that their lives are unified and continuing despite their diverse ingredients and the many changes that occur as people and societies mature and interact with one another. For him, religion in early cultures provided people with a way of relating particular entities and events to one another by means of a larger coherence, thereby helping people to give an account of themselves, their world, and their relations to and within it. Religion allowed questions

---

1 See especially E. B. Tylor, *Primitive Culture* (London: John Murray, 1903), pp. 7–31.

of why things are as they are and occur as they do to have actual or potential answers that contribute to an adequate and workable worldview.

The worldviews of early human cultures, which he called savage or primitive, contained as a crucial ingredient belief in spiritual in addition to material realities. In dreams and imagination, one experiences departures from the body, encounters with remote beings and places, and unusual and unexpected events. Death also clarifies the distinction and relation of the physical or material to the spiritual because spirit is often related to breathing and to life. It was not an unusual extension to relate the spiritual to other forms of life, both animal and vegetable, because an adequate worldview needs to take into account the particular as well as the shared, human as well as nonhuman life.

Tylor distinguished stages in the development of human cultures and their religious content. The earliest stage posited a general spiritual force that animated all beings. In a later stage, this general force became particularized in and by spiritual beings that are agents in the world, affecting entities and events in both the larger world and particular human lives. This change gave rise to polytheism, which would yield, in the next stage, to henotheism, that is, the elevation of some spiritual beings over others, and, in a final stage, to monotheism, a form of religion well-known in Western cultures.

Central to Tylor's understanding is that the religious content of human cultures, despite major changes in their developments, provides continuities both within and between stages. This is due to what he thought of as vestiges or survivals carried over from one stage of development to the next. Habits and other forms of continuity and attachment allow superseded ingredients of a culture and its religious content to persist despite change. Vestiges are also valuable for research because they offer available access to previous stages in a culture's development. Also important for Tylor is that, while the form of a religion changes primarily from simpler to more complex, the major role of religion is mainly constant, namely, to affirm the reality of the spiritual and the necessity of including the spiritual in an adequate account of the world and of a people's relations in and to it. Despite the changes brought about by cultural developments and the differences between cultures, all stages and all religiously informed cultures have the effect of providing an adequate and shared account of the world and of the place of people in it, an account that holds together both material and spiritual realities. Tylor implies, then, that an unprecedented cultural situation arises when some worldviews retain the reality of the spiritual and others do not. This implies that religious people living today have, by virtue of including the reality of the spiritual in their worldviews, more in common with other and earlier cultures than they do with their contemporaries who exclude the spiritual and are, in other words, materialists.

By seeing religion as going all the way back or down to the earliest forms of human cultures, human belief in the reality of the spiritual and forming adequate worldviews are seen as mutually supportive. This has at least two important ramifications. First, it gives to religious beliefs a basic and causative rather than a derivative, secondary, or optional standing. This poses the question of whether or not religion offers understandings of persons and their world that can adequately be replaced by materialist alternatives. Does religion offer beliefs and experiences that are necessary contributions to the formation of an adequate worldview? Second, positing an integral role of religion in human culture imputes a poignancy to Tylor's theory, since he was also aware that in his own culture technology and science were increasingly separated from religion and that this process would continue so that materialist worldviews would eventually stand as culturally dominant, leaving religion to continue only as a vestige in the culture and as less relevant to modernity than to the past.

Tylor's work, then, seems to lead us toward an unresolved uncertainty. Does human experience and awareness invite, perhaps even require, belief in the reality of the spiritual? The resources and advancements of science seem inadequate to the task of giving an adequate account of human experience generally, of human consciousness and self-consciousness particularly, and of personal and group identity and continuity over time despite changing circumstances. He seems to affirm the major importance of science for human advancement while also holding open the question of whether there are matters crucial to an adequate worldview that science and technology, with their primary orientation to the material, cannot satisfactorily provide.

The question continues today as to whether science and technology, which are greatly extended and established compared to what was the case in Tylor's day, can, along with all else that they make possible, also provide an adequate account of what is important to people, namely, a worldview that supports a workable and adequate sense of personal values, human relationships, and moral responsibilities. His distinction between people who affirm the reality of the spiritual and those who are materialists continues to stand, and it affects religious studies. It is difficult to measure in Tylor the degree of his emphasis on the role of religious beliefs and values in the present as vestiges not only carried over from the past but as providing continuity in cultural identity between the present and the past. The question is whether such important factors in human life and understanding as agency, morality, creativity, and compassion require for their status or warrant a worldview that is formed from something more or other than the material. Must an adequate worldview include the reality of something that cannot be explained by or traced back to material? While he does not resolve the tensions between views that include the reality of the spiritual and those that do not, he seems to hold out to his readers an understanding of human cultures as forming from their earliest developments worldviews that attempt to do justice to human experience and potential by including the reality of the spiritual in addition and in relation to the material.

Sigmund Freud (1856–1939)[2]

An important voice in the discussion of this third interest in religious studies is provided by Sigmund Freud. While Tylor addresses the matter more indirectly, Sigmund Freud faces it squarely. His contribution to this topic needs to be seriously considered because he recognized that religion has both deep roots in personal lives and cultures and major consequences for their development. His understanding of and critique of religion are not, then, superficial but penetrating and comprehensive. As a theorist and critic of religion, he stands alongside an equally compelling critic of religion who came at religion less from an interest in psychological or internal matters or forces than from political and economic counterparts to them, namely, Karl Marx. Both theorists pose questions that continue to provide bases for critiques of religion and the uses that are made of it, including religion's contributions to the framing of worldviews. Studying religion today means doing so in the shadow of these theorists and their progeny who make a strong case that religion in human life and societies is not superficial and casual but deeply embedded and often concealed so that it is not simply a distraction or diversion but is, or at least can be, personally and socially forceful while also, in their views, harmful. The theories of Marx and Freud created and mobilized a tradition of critique that has become prominent today and needs to be taken into account both because of its radical implications and because it reveals how religion, even if also more positively viewed, can and often does have negative consequences or augment negative tendencies in human lives and cultures. As we shall see in the second part of this book, studying religion cannot be done in disregard of critique, and, if one is inclined toward a positive view of religion, this should not be at the expense of recognizing the harm religion has done and can do.

Freud posited religion as resistant or an obstacle to human development and well-being. Religion should be seen, as also with Marx, not only as something outmoded or irrelevant but as continuing to have negative personal and social consequences. In addition, Freud's theories and analyses were deployed

---

2 See especially Sigmund Freud, "The Question of a *Weltanschauung*," Lecture XXXV in *New Introductory Lectures in Psychology*, vol. 22, (London, 1933).

in a culture increasingly attentive to personal formation, liberation, and self-actualization. Freud held open the promise of a better and brighter future for persons freed from what he considered the retarding and repressive effects of religion on them. While there is a kind of religious flavor to the Marxist future held open as a consequence of social reconstruction, and while Marxism contributed to religious thought and activity, even producing Christian Marxist theologies, Freudian theories moved from being a critique of religion to providing a kind of substitute for it, namely, psychoanalysis as a liberating and non- or anti-religious path to greater personal freedom and fulfillment. Freud posited, in relation to this program of personal actualization, the need for and role of a reconstituted worldview, one secured by science and reason and freed from what he considered to be the illusions, wishful thinking, and dependencies generated by religion that have harmful consequences for personal actualization and integrity.

A major component of Freud's theory is the power he attributed to the unconscious, which cannot itself be directly known. Its inaccessibility is due not only to its depth but also to the fact that it operates principally as a force that issues into personal life in the form of desires, instincts, drives, and fears, particularly related to sexuality. Religion has its origins to a significant degree in this deep and determining level of internal human dynamics.

A second major ingredient in Freud's theory of religion is the similarity he draws between the development of the human species and the development of individual persons. As children carry during their development misconstrued or fanciful ideas and feelings that need to be challenged and replaced as they mature, so also the human race carries from earlier stages habits of thought that impede and even harm human development. This identification of matters that retard and distort development falls out as a distinction between psychological illness and health. Isolating erroneous and retarding factors and replacing them with rationally and scientifically more reliable understandings, interpretations, and expectations is a process that is not only a replacement of the false by the true but also of psychological illness by health.

The early stages of human development, both general and individual, are heavily determined by feelings of helplessness and vulnerability. As a child looks to its parents for protection and support, the human species in its earlier stages looked to superhuman and divine protection and support. As a child matures, it needs to turn away from dependency on its parents and to take responsibility for his or her own life; so human beings also need to be freed from the need for and comforts of supernatural protectors and providers and to become self-reliant.

While the shift away from reliance on parents and gods is weighty enough on its own, its difficulty is intensified in Freud's well-known theory of the Oedipal complex. Sexual drives are not only particularity potent among the many urges in the unconscious, but they also are deeply seated and operative already in infancy. This means that the relationship of the child to its parents is driven by more than the need and desire for sustenance and security. The child desires intimacy with its mother and, as it develops, begins to recognize its father as an obstacle to and competitor for that intimacy. This process has its counterpart in the development of the species. In early societies, the desire of young men for women was thwarted by the fact that the women live under the jurisdiction of their fathers. This sets up a powerful complex of desire and resentment, resulting in the urge to be rid of the fathers. This need, which at times leads to the actual killing of the fathers or a representative of them, arouses guilt along with the prospect of release from guilt. This ambivalence, this combination of guilt and the desire for sexual satisfaction, aggravates the already difficult and complex process of moving from an early dependent immaturity to a self-reliant and liberated maturity and accounts in part for the fact that so much religion persists in human societies and so much neurosis appears in personal lives.

Religion and its roles, for Freud, are not only deeply rooted in the lives of individuals but also spread out to society, which can take on a kind of parental role for an individual, providing acceptance, protection, and reassurance at the price of conformity and repression. The frequent complicity between religion and social or political institutions arises from the need to establish order and restraints on individual needs and desires, on what Freud called the pleasure principle. He saw the need for corporate order, the reality principle, as having legitimate claims on the behaviors of persons and implied a balance between the contrary roles of these two principles in human life.

The primary means and manifestations of human maturation at both the corporate and individual levels are for Freud science and rationality. The Freudian attack on religion is so powerful, then, because, among other things, it casts religion in a negative role relative not only to individual and social but also to human and cultural advancement and well-being.

However, Freud was aware of the major contributions that religions have made in the past and continue to make in the formation of human worldviews. Religion is so recalcitrant, even in the present, because, along with what already has been said, it substantially contributes to the understandings people have of their world and of their relations to and within it. The contributions of religious beliefs to a worldview, however, are based on wishful thinking, dependencies, and illusions. This exposes a major problem because, having discredited worldviews that include religious beliefs and expectations, he does not conclude that mature people can and should live without adequate worldviews. Nor does he argue that science and rationality at the present time can provide, without religion, a worldview that is adequate.

Freud directly addressed this problem in a lecture with the title "The Question of a *Weltanschauung*." In it, he acknowledges that religion has played a major role in supplying people with a worldview and that science and rationality at present are unable to fill the lack created by the removal of religion and to provide an alternative worldview that is adequate. He fears that this present lack of adequate worldviews could support the continuing relevance of religion to contemporary human life, but he argues against granting it that role. He urges carrying on without an adequate worldview until such time when science and reason can provide one, meanwhile not allowing religion, during the interval, to fill the lack of or make up for the inadequacies of scientifically or rationally based worldviews. He calls on courage and confidence to keep people from yielding to the temptation offered by religion and its potential to provide what is lacking.

Although Freud dissociates religion from rationality by locating its origins in the unconscious, he implies that religion also has played rational roles that contributed to people's understandings of the world and their relations to and within it. Although it is not clear what all he has in mind as not yet adequately taken into account by scientifically and rationally based and framed worldviews, one could suggest that, committed as he is to a basically materialistic account of human nature and development, he could have human freedom or agency in mind since his program of maturation carried with it the prospect of fuller self-determination. But materialist accounts easily, if not unavoidably, carry deterministic implications. Also, since the reality principle, the need for limitations and directions for human needs and desires, is to some degree legitimate, the need for moral principles becomes apparent, a need that science and rationality seem unable, at least at present, to fill.

Freud's contribution to this third continuing interest in religious studies, the relation of religion to an adequate worldview, is that he does not discredit or dismiss the human need for an adequate worldview. However, he does not assign to religion the role for continuity and coherence that Tylor imputed to it if only as vestiges or survivals that are personally and culturally helpful. However, what he offers in lieu of beliefs for filling lacks left by scientific and rational accounts of humans and their world is itself a belief, namely, that persons can and should live without an adequate worldview, a belief that people can carry on unimpeded by that lack until someday, one would hope sooner rather than later, science and reason will deliver the adequate worldview that now is lacking. This appearance of belief in Freud's analysis raises the question of the personal and cultural role of nonreligious beliefs and their relation to religious beliefs, a question we shall return to later on and should consider important for religious studies and its place and role in academic culture.

Bronislaw Malinowski (1884–1942)[3]

One thing that makes Malinowski unusual among scholars in religious studies is that, while principally recognized as an anthropologist, he initially was trained in Poland as a physicist and received his doctoral degree in physics and mathematics in 1908. His background in science gave him a basis for as well as reliability regarding what could be called the scientific or technological aspects of early cultures. He went, in his studies, from physics to anthropology and did research in Australia. He is best known for having lived for two years among inhabitants of the Trobriand Islands, practicing his theory of the researcher as a participant/observer.

Likely due to his training as a scientist, Malinowski became aware that the Trobriand Islanders, who constituted an early or traditional society, did not understand their world and their relations to and within it solely in religious terms. Indeed, they were also preoccupied with the practical challenges and opportunities of daily life and developed ways of understanding them, thereby improving their own lot. Successes and setbacks were not always attributed to supernatural causes but were also treated as matters to be understood and addressed. Solutions were built on one another, so that people became more adept at responding effectively to their environment. They were even able to formulate rudimentary natural laws that allowed them to take knowledge derived from one situation and apply it to others. By means of experience, trial and error, and observation, they drew conclusions about natural phenomena and could benefit from the knowledge they acquired over time.

Such empirically and even scientifically informed understandings and practices did not, however, replace the importance of religion among these people. Their religious understandings and practices were in response to matters that their accumulated knowledge and skills could not adequately address. So, for example, their practical knowledge could help them design boats, discern weather conditions, and designate techniques that heightened success in fishing, but good weather and bountiful results, being beyond their control, were not subject to what could be called their scientific or technological knowledge and methods.

---

3 See especially Bronislaw Malinowski, *Magic, Science and Religion* (Garden City, NY: Doubleday & Company, 1948), pp. 17–36 and 85–90.

The people he observed were also capable, he found, of abstract and even hypothetical thought. They could draw maps and plan strategies. They closely observed the behaviors of animals, and, even more surprising, their observations were turned not only to practical applications concerning safety and hunting but also satisfied their curiosity concerning the differences and similarities between various animals.

As if their worlds were not already complex, these people also gave place for and practiced magic. Magic differed from what could be called scientific and rational knowledge and practice in that magical expertise was not generally shared. Magic had its own lore and practitioners. While at times it was difficult for Malinowski to clearly distinguish the scientific and rational from the magical relations of these people to their world, the distinction was often clear. For example, experience could determine what, when, and how to plant, but magic was called on to affect rainfall. Magic, in a word, is like science by addressing particular problems and needs, but unlike science because it is based not on shared experiences and reason but on particular traditions and individual gifts.

Because magic is related to spiritual powers, it also has ties to religion. Both are attuned to or respond to the spiritual powers that Malinowski called *mana*. But while magic focuses on specific needs and goals, religion is more inclusive and regularized. In other words, religion, magic, and science do not chart a chronological development but, rather, exist together in early societies. And Malinowski considered this complex cultural situation as not unique to the peoples he studied but as a likely characteristic of early cultures more generally.

The religion of these people was centered, Malinowski determined, by and on the totem, and the totem related people to one another as a whole and related them to the divine. Also, he was able to challenge the notion that early societies have a more general understanding of the divine or spiritual and move from this more general sense to identifying particular divine beings or gods. There are high gods also in early religions. Early cultures are more complex than they generally are thought to be, and in them, religion grants a unifying content to communal identity. Early religion reveals a repertoire of rituals that encompass life's important moments, such as initiations, marriage ceremonies, cleansing rites, and funeral practices.

Malinowski offered, consequently, a complex analysis of the worldview he found in early civilizations, the understandings people had of their world and their relations within and to it. Perhaps because of his own scientific interests, he was particularly drawn to what he saw as understandings that a society gains through experience, observation, and reflection. He tended to ascribe religion and magic to areas not covered adequately by what could be called scientific knowledge and technological applications. But the picture he presents is one in which all three kinds of responses or approaches are active and compatible with one another. The coherence or continuity in their worldviews, despite the complexity and even division between kinds of knowledge and practice, may be attributable to two causes. One of them may have been the primary belief, confirmed by religious understandings and practices, that persons and the society are unified. This religiously-based sense of a unified people, centered in and by the totem and related thereby to one another and to the divine, could have a centripetal effect that moderated the centrifugal effects that diverse kinds of understandings and actions could have had. A second and perhaps more important factor contributing to a sense of coherence and continuity despite differences and changes may well have been that, as Malinowski points out, the people he observed did not make a deep and sharp distinction between the sacred and the profane. The profane was, Malinowski concluded, not a threat for these people and, even more, not an evil. The profane was viewed in a more neutral way as potential or as unorganized. It was viewed in a way similar to how moderns sometimes view the secular, namely, as neutral or not religiously designated.

Malinowski's contribution to this chapter on religion and worldviews is important because he calls into question the assumption that early societies lived in a unified world because everything that existed or occurred was interrelated by means of religious beliefs and practices. His notice and account of what he identified as scientifically formed understandings and practices were grounded in his training as a physicist and must therefore be taken seriously. The complex world of early societies anticipated, then, what we take to be a particularly, even uniquely, noticeable mark of late modern Western culture, namely, an increasing separation and eventual tension between scientifically and religiously framed understandings and practices. Indeed, our own worldviews are less complex than were those of societies observed by Malinowski because magic, having suffered discrediting in modernity by both science and religion, holds only a minor or marginal place, if place at all, in modern Western culture. Malinowski's observations and theories indicate that the separations and tensions between religion and science that are such visible aspects of modern Western culture need not be attributed to the nature of science, on the one hand, and of religion, on the other. The separation and tension may arise as much, if not more, from the loss we have suffered of a sense of personal and cultural wholeness and have substituted for it a primary sense of individuality, difference, and even opposition. It may also be due to a cultural view of religion that construes it as disconnected from and even opposed to science and rationality and a view of science and rationality as fully adequate for understanding what it means to be human and what our relations to and within our world can or should be.

Mircea Eliade (1907–1986)[4]

Although Mircea Eliade spent part of his career in Paris and is well known in the United States for his contributions to the study of religion while on the faculty of the University of Chicago from the mid-fifties until his death thirty years later, it is important to remember that he was born and raised in Romania. This is because Romania is a country that, like others in the region, was subjected to many difficult times imposed on it by the economic and political interests of more powerful surrounding nations. Deeply embedded in Eliade's work, then, is an awareness of the damages caused by war and the dominance of power. It is also important to keep in mind that Eliade, while a scholar, also achieved, especially in Romania, recognition as a novelist, and aesthetic and narrative interests play roles in his research and understanding of religion.

Like his older contemporary, the Dutch scholar of religion Gerardus van der Leeuw, who was also drawn to aesthetics, Eliade was phenomenological in method. This means, first, that he did not think of religion as having its basis or origins in something else, whether sociological or psychological, but that, while related to such other factors, it must be viewed in its own terms. Second, a phenomenological approach is one that sees a religion as constituting a more or less coherent whole. When a segment of a religion is isolated for study, a rite, for example, or a totem, it should be treated not in isolation but as part of what comprehends it. This approach to the study of a religion is consistent with what Eliade takes a religion primarily to be, namely, the provider of a unified, meaningful, and vital world. Third, a phenomenological approach to religious studies implies that a religion, before it is analyzed, should be, as Weber proposed with his concept of *Verstehen*, understood. This understanding has somewhat the status of an intuition, something van der Leeuw called empathy. It is also suggested by Malinowski's description of the student of religion as a participant as well as an observer.

Like others we have considered, Eliade finds religion most fully present in the early stages of human life, but, unlike some others, he did not see religion as something that humans should or need to outgrow as they develop. Like Jung, he discerned patterns or archetypes that various religions share, that reveal similarities between differing religions, and that continue to play a role in our own time and place. These patterns or archetypes structure the plots of myths, and myths give rise to powerful symbols. But unlike

---

4 See especially Mircea Eliade, *Patterns in Comparative Religion*. Trans. Rosemary Sheed. (London: Sheed and Ward, 1958), pp. 1–33.

Jung, Eliade did not locate these patterns and archetypes primarily in the unconscious. Rather, they are perceived as coming from beyond, affecting human life, and manifested in certain events and objects. The word he used for such manifestations is *hierophany*, the appearance of the sacred in something particular.

The sacred is, as for others such as Durkheim, a central concept for Eliade. For religious people, the sacred is the real; it is recurring, dependable, and meaning-granting. It is most commonly associated by religious people temporally with beginnings and spatially with the center. This is why many myths and rituals deal with origins or cosmogony, and this is also why, whether located in Delphi, Jerusalem, or Mecca, the sacred place is the center or axis mundi of the world.

The human world is ordered temporally by the distinction and relation between the beginning and the subsequent. And the human world is ordered spatially by a relation between its center and peripheries. The further a person is from the center or from the beginning the less meaningful or whole a person's or people's world and view of it becomes. This is why myths and rituals are so important. They invoke the beginning and relate people to the center. Cosmogonic myths are particularly important, as are also pilgrimage sites.

Eliade was especially captivated by the rhythmic quality of traditional societies. Repeatedly, religious people return to the center or the beginnings by means of myths and rituals, since temporal and spatial distances result in the loss of meaningfulness, unity, and vitality. Religious rituals and myths are regularly repeated. Because temporal and spatial distances create disorientation, their inevitable results must be countered by repeated returns to the beginnings and to the center.

Since recurrence or rhythm is so basic for religion, it is not surprising that natural phenomena are also important for religions—seasonal changes, the phases of the moon, and transitions in personal and collective life, such as initiations, weddings, births, burials, and coronations. Indeed, history, the sense of time as unidirectional and forward-moving, has religiously an uncertain and even questionable status. A remarkable occurrence in the history of religions, for Eliade, is the shift of emphasis by ancient Hebrews from time as primarily cyclical to time as primarily linear. Historical time, the least susceptible to *hierophany*, became for Judaism and Christianity the most important. But for Eliade the identification of religion with history is also the reason why there is so much alienation, skepticism, and violence in the modern West. Still, Judaism and Christianity also resemble other religions by retaining strong cyclical elements that lead to and restore beginnings and the center and that, by doing so, counter some of the negative consequences of linear time and spatial distance.

While Eliade displays an emphasis on the sacred, it is important for understanding his theories to notice the somewhat muted but nonetheless primary role taken in his work by the profane. He says, for example, that the first possible definition of the sacred is that it is the opposite of the profane. That is, the sacred, although real, is also transcendent and variously manifested. The profane, in contrast, is relatively constant and is something we already know; awareness of it is shared, especially in the modern West. Violence, dislocation, fragmentation, meaninglessness, despair, and all the rest that goes into a description of the human situation in the modern West are due to or identifiable as the profane. The sacred is first of all profane's contrary; it grants wholeness, meaningfulness, restoration, and location. Modern Westerners retain, no matter how deeply affected they are by the force of linear history and the dominance of the profane, a sense of how things really are or ought to be. They continue to have a longing for and seek out occasions for reorientation and return. The study of religion, like the study of or exposure to art, is, then, a revealing, restorative, and reorienting practice. If aesthetic or other experiences give us the sense of a whole and of significance, it is because of the presence in a work of art of the sacred. The problem is that modern Westerners identify with linear historical advance in order to acquire power, to exploit nature, and to subjugate other peoples. Embracing history as warranting power is characteristic of and appealing to people for whom the course of history has been beneficial.

There is a strong philosophical, even metaphysical, aspect to Eliade's work, therefore. Rather than reduce our being in a world primarily to material survival, he relates it to meaning as a comprehensive and supportive whole. He proposed that this whole or this sustaining worldview is granted to a person or people in three ways. It is granted temporally by people being restored to the fullness of that which gave rise to what exists. It is granted spatially by providing or restoring to people an awareness of a center, an axis mundi. And it is granted by enabling people to relate objects and events in their world to archetypes, myths, or ritual patterns. Signs of and access to the sacred are never lost in a society or culture no matter how given over it may be to the profane. Indeed, the profane, by means of its negative effects, arouses awareness of and a search for the sacred. Implied by his theory is that anything meaningful that occurs in the world is meaningful because, however implicitly, it is actually or potentially related to something more real, such as origin, center, or archetype. Wherever there is meaning, in other words, there is something traceable to religion, however muted, integrated, or implicit it may be. Religion and the study of religion provide an understanding of the kind of worldviews that are required if people are to be delivered from what they suffer, namely, the alienating, dislocating, and enervating effects of the profane.

Clifford Geertz (1926–2006)[5]

After serving as a member of the Anthropology departments at the University of California at Berkeley, the University of Chicago, and Oxford University, Clifford Geertz came to the Institute for Advanced Studies at Princeton in 1970 and spent the rest of his career there. He did field work in Java and Bali, and he is well known for his comparative study of Islam in Indonesia and Morocco. He is particularly well known for his emphasis on the role of religion in providing a society with an inclusive and coherent culture. This means that, while not ignoring distinct religious beliefs, practices, and feelings, his interests were also linguistic, textual, and literary.

Like Max Weber, Geertz was interested in how religion motivates and directs people, but he was also influenced by Ludwig Wittgenstein's theory of forms of life as having a centripetal direction and providing people with a distinct or particular language that, while carrying family resemblances to other languages, has an integrity and coherence of its own. Like Weber, too, he, along with Eliade, emphasized that particular items within a culture or religion had to be understood in their context as a whole. Like them, too, he believed that an outsider could not understand as fully as could an insider the meaning or purpose of some particular aspect of a religion. He therefore distinguished between two kinds of understanding, "emic," which is an understanding available to a participant in a religion, and "etic," which is an understanding available to an outsider or observer.

While Geertz related religion closely with culture, he also made distinctions between the two. Religion provides understandings of the world that form a comprehensive whole in which people locate themselves and to which they feel related. Religion has a unifying consequence, relating metaphysical, physical, and ethical matters to one another. It also relates the comprehensive, even the ultimate, to the practical, and relates the cosmological to the incidental. The meanings and motivations provided by religion are treated as factual and become ingrained in people's lives like a second nature. While religion requires a culture and is required by a culture, culture tends to relate to more particular matters and to be more subject to change and internal diversity. This is why a single religion can be integral for cultures that are in many respects unlike one another, as are the cultures of Indonesia and Morocco, both of which are primarily Islamic. Such differences reveal the distinction between religion and culture even though, practically, people living within them may not be able so easily to point to that distinction.

---

5 See especially Clifford Geertz, "Religion as a Cultural System" in *The Interpretation of Cultures: Selected Essays* (New York: HarperCollins Publishers, 1973), pp. 87–125.

For Geertz, to be human is to require a *Weltanschauung* of some kind, a meaningful world and meaningful relations to and within it. This does not mean that a person or a people need to be always conscious of living in such a world or need to be able to articulate its elements or defend its viability. It also does not mean that this worldview stands ready adequately to account for or to explain everything that exists or occurs. The worldview must be coherent or complete enough to be sustained even if something particular is dissonant within it. Indeed, an adequate worldview is one that can house dissonance. A viable religious culture is one that provides a meaningful whole that is not dismantled by the unexpected or unexplained. The problematic particular is housed, however uneasily, within a sustained and reassuring whole. It could be said, in fact, that a religious culture does not so much explain things as give participants the assurance that whatever exists or occurs has a place in and relates meaningfully to the whole if not obviously then potentially.

Religion and culture, then, although in separable ways that are not always distinguished, cooperate in providing an adequate worldview, that is, a sense of wholeness in which people understand themselves to be meaningfully included. It may not be too much to say, however, that in his work the relation of religion and culture to one another lies somewhat along the lines of the relation of what is stable and essential in the meaningfulness that people have in relation to their worlds to what is particular, changeable, or scattered. There is an analogous relation, it seems, between the mixture of the continuous or transcendent and the various and changeable in the relation of religion and culture to one another and the mixture of both in language. Language, in order to serve, also needs to combine elements that give it stability, even invariability, with elements that allow for changes and individual uses. While not the same as the distinction for structural linguists between *langue* and *parole*, the distinction between what is stabilizing in culture and what is variable and changeable resembles it as well. The distinction and interdependence of religion and culture in Geertz's work seems to resemble the play within linguistic theories between, to use another set of distinctions, repertoire and performance.

At the risk of overstretching his theories to address the separation in late modern Western culture between the religious or personal and the nonreligious and public, it may be fair to say that for Geertz neither of these separated realms can be called on to provide by itself a worldview that is coherent, adequate, and workable. This is implied by the basic distinction he makes between culture and religion. A worldview in his view houses two distinguishable parts, and neither, by implication, is able to complete the task by itself. It can be inferred, therefore, that attempts made by those who identify with one or the other of the separated realms and try to form from that one side an adequate worldview is asking too much of it. Indeed, there is no lack today of attempts to do just that, and they persist in the face of an inability to shape one realm to cover the whole. What is needed, if an engagement between them is to occur, is a recognition that an adequate and shared worldview cannot emerge if one of the two realms is called on to provide the whole.

Conclusion

Although varying in the extent of its role in their work, these five scholars in religious studies all call attention to or focus on the need people have for an adequate understanding of their world and of their relations in and to it. That is, people identify and interpret particular things and events in their world not only as isolated or in relation to one another but also, perhaps more importantly, in relation to a more inclusive framework or whole. Indeed, there is reciprocity between particulars and the framework that grants people a relatively coherent and stable, although also complex and changing, worldview. They encounter new things, but they relate them to what they previously have encountered, what they expect to encounter, and some larger framework or actual or potential meaning. The worldviews with which people live may not be conscious; they often function in an implicit way so that responses to particular events or objects are taken to be obvious or natural. When people encounter others who do not share their worldview, they may become more aware that they understand and evaluate things in a particular way and may even begin to question their own views. As likely, they will tend to dismiss other views as less adequate, accurate, or tenable than their own. The need for such a comprehensive and coherent understanding of a person's or group's world becomes increasingly apparent as modernity progresses because people find themselves in a world in which important matters are increasingly unrelated and even contrary to one another, such as science and religion, personal and social interests, internal feelings and needs and external environments, and particular experiences and a unifying understanding of them. These five examples of religious studies relate being religious to the need for a comprehensive understanding that can grant people a world that is, to a significant and adequate degree, unified, and enabling them to have meaningful relations in and to it. Although they are not in agreement as to whether religion still can and should contribute to the formation of adequate worldviews in the present culture, they do not see the need for them to have been outgrown. Those who doubt or discredit the continuing role of religion in providing an adequate worldview are faced with either the question of what, then, will replace what religion for others helps to provide or with the question of whether a worldview without religious beliefs or a substitute for them can be adequate.

I think that it is helpful and possible for easing the difference created by the separation in the culture of religious from nonreligious interests to take, as a starting point, the inference drawn from the work of Clifford Geertz at the end of the section on him, namely, that neither realm in the divided situation has in itself the potential for supplying an adequate worldview. A second point with which to start, in my opinion, is by identifying a category that would stand between a religiously based and a nonreligiously, secular, or materialistically based worldview.

It was suggested, in the description of his work given earlier, that Bronislaw Malinowski distinguished three and not two areas of interest within the early culture he studied. Between the two readily distinguishable areas of interest, practical, material, or technological, on the one hand, and religious, on the other, there existed a third or middle cultural interest, namely, magic. Like the practical or empirical side, magic was attentive to practical and particular needs and goals. However, it also resembled or was related to the religious side by its identification with the exceptional or mysterious. Due to this mediation, the culture, while complex, was more unified than it otherwise would be. He also avoided the practice of defining or identifying the sacred in religious life and thought by projecting the profane in opposition to the sacred. I would take the proposals of Malinowski as contributing factors to the possibility of framing or forming a more coherent and shared worldview.

A place and role similar to those given by Malinowski to magic can, I think, be given to nonreligious beliefs. To consider this proposal, namely, that nonreligious beliefs can stand between religious beliefs and the attempt to project an adequate worldview on the basis of empirical and rational certainty, we need first to be clear as to what is meant by beliefs.

Beliefs stand between shared knowledge and religious faith. Unlike knowledge, beliefs do not have the support of what is generally taken, because of rational or empirical support, to be irrefutable. And unlike religious faith, nonreligious beliefs do not carry with them the assurances of divine or transcendent origin or authority. Beliefs can be thought to be similar to knowledge in that they apply to matters that are concrete and shared and similar to religious beliefs by not relying for support on rational or empirical confirmation. Nonreligious, like religious beliefs, can be held firmly and contribute to the worldviews of persons or groups by providing principles that grant meaning, values, and moral norms.

Beliefs, whether religious or nonreligious, are necessary for an adequate worldview because of the four components necessary for adequacy. The first concerns other people, what to expect of them or how to interpret them.

Should they be taken as trustworthy or as prone to evil? Are they fixed or changeable? Are they particular or definable by their class, gender, race, or ethnicity? The second concerns the temporal processes in which one participates or by which one is affected, social and ontological events and their causes and consequences. Are they negatively or positively related to human well-being or should they be resisted or altered? The third matter of concern is the conditions under and with which one must live, the environment of a life. Given these conditions, what is possible and what is not possible to occur or to do? What are the limits and potentials of the situation in which personal and social life is carried on? Finally, a concern is for determining what is worthy of one's attention and how it should be understood and evaluated. In order to arise in the morning and to enter a viable and workable world, a person must have answers to the questions raised by each of these four components: what other people are like, to what the processes by which one is involved are leading, the favorable and supportive or restricting and deleterious effects on a person of the conditions of one's surroundings, and to what a person should pay attention or direct one's efforts. The answers given or assumed to these four sets of questions are required for a person's arising each morning to an adequately meaningful and workable world. These answers are beliefs or rest on beliefs. Not everyone will agree with the answers to these questions or the evidence and arguments offered to confirm them.

Nonreligious believers can have commendable attributes. They can be generous, compassionate, concerned for the well-being of others, and faithful and dependable to their commitments and responsibilities, even more so than religious people. Religious believers can have much in common with them, if they have similar beliefs, even though they will attribute them to transcendent, religiously authoritative, or spiritual sources and warrants. Religious believers may consider the beliefs of nonreligious people to be insufficiently supported or as unrecognized vestiges or survivals of religious beliefs, but they can, meanwhile, recognize commonality with them.

Religious studies can contribute to the formation of adequate and workable worldviews by taking into more consideration the important and unifying roles and effects of nonreligious beliefs for mediating between secular or materialist worldviews and those that rest on beliefs that find their origins or supports in religion. Religious studies can contribute more fully to the task of providing adequate and shared worldviews if the value and utility of nonreligious beliefs are recognized both by themselves and by the mediation they provide between a religiously derived belief system and attempts to understand the world in terms based on understandings dependent finally on some kind or degree of materialism. More will be said about culturally relevant nonreligious beliefs and their relation to religious studies in the second part of this guide.

Part Two

THEORETICAL

Chapter 5

THE OBJECT OF RELIGIOUS STUDIES

Having identified three interests or topics in religious studies to which notable scholars for the last two centuries have given consideration, a basic question arises concerning what marks are adequate and necessary to warrant referring to a person or a people as religious. The scholars whose work we have considered do not shape their work by first forming an answer to the question of what constitutes being religious and then applying that answer to their study of people. While some come closer than others to provide an answer to this question, it is less than central for all of them because, given their positions largely in the human or social sciences, they are primarily attentive less to what religion is and more attentive to its locations and roles in people's lives, its relations to human needs and potentials. Because they begin more with human needs and potentials than with religion more fully understood, their understandings of religion are focused and partial. As we turn now less to historical and more to theoretical matters, it becomes urgent to begin with the question of what being religious consists, by what being religious is constituted. While one would think that anyone working in religious studies would have addressed this matter, it seems seldom to arise, and it has not produced a shared answer. Many definitions have been offered, but none has become standard.

One reason for the difficulty is that religion, as we have seen, takes many forms and has many roles. This diversity makes it difficult to have agreement about what allows some people and not others to be designated as religious. A second reason is that there are among scholars who study religion disagreements concerning religion's standing. Is religion primary and generative in human lives and cultures or is it secondary, a product or symptom of something nonreligious? Are religious practices, feelings, and beliefs too embedded in other aspects of human lives and cultures to be separated out as being something other or more than those factors? A third difficulty is that uncertainty arises concerning the value of religion in and for human lives and societies. If religion does play a role in human life, is it a good or at least a neutral thing, or is it something that is questionable or even objectionable? Enough evidence can be mustered to support both positive and negative views of religion, and it is not surprising to find that at times one can encounter a scholar of religion who seems to have a negative view of it and its consequences for human well-being.

As both a cause and a result of the uncertainty or lack of agreement as to what religion is, we find that the terms "religion" and "religious" are variously used. This variance in usage increases doubt that there is something sufficiently stable, recurring, or identifiable in the variety of usages to warrant the expectation of a shared and adequate definition. We should first look more closely at the reasons for doubting the dependability or usefulness of these terms before taking up the task of stabilizing their meaning and referents. At the least, the level of uncertainty and the potential threat to religious studies created by the lack of a shared understanding of religion should be reduced as much as possible.

I

We should begin by retrieving a point made earlier in this book, namely, that the location of religious studies in institutions that are not themselves religiously identifiable is between religious and nonreligious understandings of religion. This point led to the assertion that religious studies should not be identified wholly with one or the other of these contraries but as standing between and drawing from each of them. Religious studies is located between the study of religion in religiously identifiable locations and nonreligiously identified academic departments. I ventured the opinion that the secular side is becoming or already now is the more prominent of the two. I ventured the further opinion that the social sciences, which form the most likely locations for the nonreligious study of religion, have been increasingly affected by theoretical and methodological materialism. To the degree that these opinions are warranted, the threat it poses for religious studies is that "religion" comes to be regarded as reducible to something else. When materialist assumptions are active, the assumption that religion is recognizably a separable object of study can be taken as itself religious, that is, as constituting a form of religious advocacy. On the other side, religion is studied from a position that is itself religious, and such a position tends to focus too sharply on one religion obviating the need to define religion as manifesting itself variously. Religious studies cannot address the question of its object by starting out from a position determined by or identified with either of these contrary sides. While related to both, it also differs from them. At a minimum, religious studies must affirm, on the one side, that religion is plural and intertwined with human needs and potentials, but it cannot assume that religion is wholly created and determined by them. It needs, in its orientation to the confessional side, also to affirm that religion is something particular that can be and often is primary and causative for human lives and cultures and is not adequately regarded when treated as secondary and derived from something nonreligious.

While over-simplified, it is helpful, for the sake of clarity, to identify the assumption that religion is not something distinguishable and worth studying in and by itself as more or less noticeably a materialist assumption and that it is possible to say that assumptions of that kind are increasingly pervasive in academic culture. The increasingly dominant position of materialist methods and assumptions in academic culture has at least three causes or results. The first is that materialism provides a shared basis for research, scholarly exchange, and agreement. Matters that can most productively be pursued and debated are those that, it is thought, can be traced to their simplest form, stripped, in other words, of their putative value or meaning and ultimately traceable to matter and energy or power. The need for a common discourse based on shared procedural and theoretical norms causes and supports the emergence of materialist assumptions concerning what can profitably be talked about, what can be studied, or what actually or with sufficient certainty is the case.

Another reason why materialism has become increasingly pervasive is the prestige in the academy that the natural sciences have achieved as paradigmatic for what research and knowledge basically and intrinsically are and should be. The scientific method, as earlier suggested, consists primarily of two moves. The first is to strip what is examined of existing understandings and evaluations of it, to see it as much as possible as it actually is. The second is to reduce what is examined as much as possible to its simplest level, its constitutive components. There is nothing wrong with this procedure. Indeed, it has been and will continue to be not only productive but also necessary. What is questionable is the extension of this way of viewing and doing things into a wider understanding not only of what some but rather of what all forms of scholarly activity consist and even of what the world in which we live and of our relations within and to it consist. The specialized method and assumption for doing research in a laboratory has been extended not only to become a governing understanding of research and knowledge in general but also increasingly a shared cultural assumption.

The third reason why materialism has become so pervasive in current academic culture derives from the position of the social sciences between the natural sciences and the humanities. It is not surprising that in the mid-nineteenth century, the social sciences, particularly sociology, should arise because of the profound social changes occurring from increasingly material determinations, including urbanization, industrialization, and the means of transportation and communication. It is also not surprising that the social or human sciences should be influenced by the rapid rise in importance of science and technology. Matter and energy or power gained prominence in methods for studying human behaviors and societies. There is no question about the advances that can be made by applying scientific procedures to the study of human life, both corporate and individual. But this means that the social sciences, although standing between the natural sciences and the humanities, defer more to the natural sciences than to the humanities and transfer scientific interests to the humanities rather than humanistic interests to the sciences. While departments of religious studies generally were placed in the humanities division of the academic structure, by the closing decades of the twentieth century the humanities became increasingly affected by the social sciences and shaped by methods and interests derived from them. The means by which the humanities became increasingly affected by the social sciences are many, but the most notable forms of influence, as earlier suggested, were Marxist and Freudian. Traditionally, the humanities were custodians and apologists of what was taken to be, if not transcendental, at least normative, that is, culturally worthy of attention, admiration, and aspiration. The humanities thus played a kind of moral or spiritual role in the academy, and their loose associations with religion, maintained by academic traditions well into the twentieth century, was articulated in the Victorian period and largely taken for granted.

Materialism, particularly in Marxian and Freudian forms, sponsored a critical approach to the objects of humanistic studies that treated them as concealing something more real and less deserving of the cultural honorifics of "high" and normative. This critical approach had significant consequences for the assessment of and attitude toward high culture because it exchanged admiration or advocacy for suspicion. By the close of the twentieth century, high culture came increasingly to be treated as concealing and even justifying something more basic, causative, and questionable. The humanities became less oriented to questions of what it is good for us to be, admire, or emulate, less oriented toward furthering and refining norms and ideals, and more critical of high culture as concealing or warranting social, economic, and political group- or self-interests. This is not to say that this critical stance was unjustified; it sharpened awareness that cultural constructions can repress, exclude, or neglect as well as include, refine, and enhance the valid and vital interests of people. However, as it turned out, this shift in attitude elevated and strengthened something else, namely, the critic who now possessed the confidence to question and even subvert the implicit authority of culture and its icons. Students were, even if only implicitly, led and empowered to position themselves not in an attitude of respect and appreciation for culture traditionally secured but in a position of critical superiority or exception to it, exposing what in any particular instance is the case, especially political and economic or material interests.

Like the humanities more generally, religious studies had no answer to this powerful reversal that turned what largely was thought admirable, edifying, and normative into something secondary, questionable, and even objectionable. This shift in stance in humanities departments, including religious studies, caused tensions within their faculties. These tensions were increased by the fact that the humanities and religious studies had been and to a degree continue to be oriented to traditions, in other words, to the past, to texts, and to ideals or beliefs while the increasingly materialist academic culture and its critiques turned attention primarily toward the present day and the future and toward tangible objects and forces.

One would think that religious studies in this context of increasing materialist interests and methods would look for support to religious sources established in or connected to the academic structure. But two things made this difficult. First, departments of religious studies wanted primarily to have enfranchisement in the arts and sciences, and to do so they had to create a distance from interests that were religiously sponsored. In addition, another change, a less noticeable but still very important one, occurred in many religiously identifiable locations of the study of religion. Scholars of religion who carried and applied religious beliefs to their studies concluded that religion should be identified and understood as contrary not only to modern Western culture but also to human culture more generally. In other words, influential religious advocates agreed with materialistically grounded critics of religion by promoting a separation between religion, particularly in its traditional or institutional forms, and modern culture. Religion came more to be seen as contrary to rather than embedded in and to some degree positively related to modern Western culture. Since the rise of religious studies was related to modernity, especially, as we have seen, to Romanticism, this separation of institutional or traditional forms of religion from the academic study of religion, or religious studies, intensified the discontinuity between them. These understandings of religion contrary to modernity could make common cause with newly sharpened critical stances toward modernity in the humanities and social sciences, particularly in Marxist forms. They could agree on seeing modernity as a product of human self- or group interest in and thirst for power. A conclusion to be drawn from this context or background, one important to what follows, is that religious studies lost real or possible support from both sides, from confessional or ecclesiastical, especially Christian interests, and from departments in the humanities and social sciences increasingly determined by materialist methods and assumptions.

These shifts of interest served to alter the standing and role of religious studies in nonreligiously affiliated institutions. As described in the first chapter of this book, the place and role of religious studies in the academic structure was altered by the rapid founding and enlarging of departments of religion after the Second World War. For reasons given there, this rise and establishment was prominently, if not dominantly, shaped by the hiring of faculty for these departments who were trained in institutions of graduate studies in religion that were religiously identifiable, especially as Protestant. In the closing decades of the twentieth century, departments of religious studies were marked by an increasingly noticeable difference or tension between these contrary orientations, one to the relation of religious studies to nonreligious academic interests and the other to its relation to a religiously based or shaped study of religion. The direction of religious studies as I have traced it was and continues to be affected, especially in nonreligiously identifiable institutions, by the steady increase in religious studies as related to and even determined by materialist methods and interests, especially in the social sciences. What this situation seems to call for is a recognition of the need for a renewed, while also updated, orientation of religious studies to methods and interests that are identifiable as religiously based.

II

Keeping this complex and changing background in mind, we can turn now to the task of identifying and describing the object of religious studies without depending on primary support for this task either from other departments in arts and sciences or confessional forms of religious, especially Christian, studies. As suggested, we should begin with acknowledging the skepticism that inevitably affects discussions of this question. No better place for doing that is a conclusion concerning this task offered by Jonathan Z. Smith, a conclusion that is widely known, clearly articulated, and, for many, influential. It was widely disseminated by his essay, "Religion, Religions, and Religious."[1] Smith argues that these terms have an uncertain status because of their lack of reliable referents. Their force and meaning are derived less from that to which they refer than from the interests of the persons using them. What they designate is determined by what those who use them want to accomplish. Smith's suggestion that the category of religion, because its

---

1 See Jonathan Z. Smith, "Religion, Religions, and Religious" in Mark Taylor (ed.) *Critical Terms for Religious Studies* (Chicago: The University of Chicago Press, 1998), pp. 269–284.

object or referent is not secure, lacks a shared or standard meaning and force cannot be gainsaid. One reason for difficulty in defining these terms is, as was earlier mentioned, that people, including scholars, use them variously. But one senses that something more is at stake here. Smith's approach to religious studies is primarily sociological. For example, his account of sacred places is consistent with the topic of human place-relations when addressed by sociologists, namely, that sacred places derive their standing as a consequence of significance projected on them by their users.[2] It is not surprising, then, that he would see "religion" and "religious" as terms that acquire their standing not because of that to which they refer but because of how people, especially scholars, deploy them. Religion, religious, and religions are terms, then, that carry the meanings determined by the various interests and goals of religion scholars.

While the meaning of these terms is certainly affected by how they are used, I would also say that, despite variety of usages, we should not give up the attempt to propose for general agreement what it is to which we refer when we use these terms. We need not attribute their meaning solely or primarily to the meaning the user imparts to them. To start with, we can say that the term "religious" has a measure of stability because it is used to refer to some things or some people and not to others. This is because there are some behaviors, ideas, and, especially, people that warrant such a designation and others who do not. These terms have usefulness and even necessity not only or primarily because people use them but also because they signify a detectable and important distinction between some kinds of people and others. Uses of the term "religious" may vary, but they carry a degree of stability mainly because they stand as contraries to "nonreligious." To begin, then, we can say that when someone encounters the adjective "religious" as referring to some people and not to others, that person can have some certainty concerning what is meant. The distinction is recognizable and meaningful.

We should also keep in mind that defining "religion" and "religious" is made more difficult than it needs to be because definitions are at times too narrowly and rigidly put forward and thereby cannot take into account differences and complexities. They are often too narrow to house variations and even tensions within religion. This is particularly true of the first of them, "religion." It appears to be precise because it is abstract and single, and it has academic standing because of support granted to it by

---

2 See, for example, Irwin Altman and Setha M. Low (eds.), *Place Attachments* (New York and London: Planum, 1992) and John R. Gold and Jacquelin Burgess (eds.), *Valued Environments* (London: Allen & Unwin, 1982).

departments of religious studies formed on the assumption that religions, such as Islam, Buddhism, or Christianity, are entities that stand out as objects of study. The term is deployed to create something single and constant out of something that is complex, various, changing, and even conflicted. The questionable uses and standing of "religion," therefore, warrant a shift in attention from "religion" to "religious" because it is less abstract and more flexible. In addition, "religious" has a contrary that stabilizes its meaning, namely, "nonreligious," while "religion" has no comparable contrary by which to be stabilized. I think I know what someone means when they refer to a person, group, activity, or interest as "religious," in part because I know what is meant by referring to something or someone as nonreligious. Something recognizable and meaningful is indicated when one person self-refers to or is named by others as religious and when someone else is identified as nonreligious. "Religion," if useful at all, can perhaps be retained as an inclusive and abstract term that unifies some of the characteristics to what or to whom we refer in more particular ways as "religious," but if retained, "religion" should be seen as a general concept derived from and dependent on particulars that can be given to the adjective "religious," such as beliefs, objects, or practices, as particulars that can be identified with religious people. What makes a religion religious? The best answer to that question, it seems to me, is "religious persons," and the question arises as to what we mean when we identify ourselves or others as "religious." The basis for stabilizing the referent for religious studies is religious people, and the question then becomes what characteristics of a person or people are adequate and necessary to warrant identifying some but not all persons or peoples as "religious."

However, while religious people share religious-making characteristics, by no means can it be said that all religious people are basically alike. Our definition of "religious," then, must account for the ways not only that religious people are like one another but also ways by which they significantly differ from one another without thereby forfeiting their status as religious persons. We need a definition that distinguishes religious from nonreligious people and also accounts for why religious people differ not only from nonreligious people and people of other religions but also often from people of the same religion. We should now turn to the task of providing a definition that, by meeting these requirements, will serve.

III

One thing implied by using the term "religious" is that the persons or people referred to are aware of, take an interest in, or are oriented toward what they take to be meaningful and forceful but that cannot be humanly understood or controlled. Unlike objects of attention or interest that, while not presently, may someday be understood or controlled, those of religious people are taken to be beyond or of a kind that defies being understood or controlled. The first characteristic of religious people is that they take seriously what they acknowledge cannot be understood or controlled, what stands as distinguishable from and even contrary to what humans do or possibly can understand or control. The category of what cannot be understood or controlled is neither empty nor conjectural. Religious people have a repertoire of ideas, terms, and attitudes concerning what cannot be understood or controlled. Religious studies, then, draws attention to beliefs, actions, and feelings that refer to or are responses to what, to put it broadly, cannot be understood or controlled. The inability to understand or control that to which religious people direct their attention need not and usually does not reduce for them its standing or significance. The human inability to understand or control is a sign or result of the status and nature of what cannot be understood or controlled.

While it at times is taken as an adequate description of what is meant by "religious persons," this first factor by itself is not adequate to convey what is meant when referring to oneself or others as religious. It is too broad and vague. A second factor is necessary when adequately referring to a person or people as religious, namely, that for them what cannot be understood or controlled is accessible within the human world, whether more generally or more specifically, whether directly or indirectly, or whether in the present, the future, or the past. Despite variation, this second constitutive factor is that, for religious persons, there is something actual or potential in their world that allows them to have or seek contact, even relations, with what cannot be understood or controlled. To view it from the other side, the first factor, what cannot be understood or controlled, is, due to this second factor, made identifiable, accessible, and to some degree knowable to people in events and/or sites within the human world. However, the events or sites that make what cannot be understood or controlled available do not cancel or dilute its standing but are affected by it while not being substitutes for it.

The third factor that is implied by referring to oneself or others as religious is that this, which cannot be understood or controlled and with which persons or a people can have a degree of access or contact, is beneficially relevant to and consequential for their well-being, for their understandings of their world, and for their relations to and within that world. The consequences of relations with what cannot be understood or controlled for the well-being of religious persons or peoples can be occasional and partial or thorough-going and radical. It can be supplemental to what already is taken to be the world and relations within and to it; it can be a corrective to what otherwise would be taken to be the case; or it can cause a shift so that the person or group is aligned now not with the world as otherwise encountered but with the world that stands in a differing and even contrary way to what was formerly or otherwise the case. This third factor in identifying some people as religious has consequences that, while they may be complex, are finally positive. It provides, among many other things, stability, significance, and purpose to people's worlds and lives. However various and unlike one another the behaviors and beliefs of religious people may be, they affect religious people's relations in and to their world in ways that are for them beneficial. Religious persons or groups live in a world, at least to some noticeable degree positively affected by their relations to what cannot be understood or controlled that to some degree and in some way is made accessible to them. While also true of the other factors that go into designating a person or group as religious, this factor complicates the precision of the designation because it relates to personal, social, and cultural conditions. While there is also similarity and relations in what it is that is humanly beneficial in what is received, it will also be various. These various applications of what is received cannot be brought into a category that is shared. It is tempting, therefore, to isolate and marginalize them, but it needs also to be said that being religious includes kinds of human needs and potentials that give particularity to being religious. There is personal, group, and cultural variety to what is taken to be human needs, potentials, and well-being, and this variety is not incidental. It accounts greatly for the differences not only between people of differing religions but also between people of the same religion.

As though this description of religious persons or peoples were not complex enough, it must also be said that it is not the case that all three of these religion-making characteristics will be for any religious person or group of equal importance. Indeed, it appears that one of the three will, perhaps necessarily, be dominant for any religious person or group and that the dominant characteristic will subject and deform the other two characteristics of the religious system toward itself. All three factors must be present in order to refer to a person or group as religious, but one of the three will likely, let us venture to say inevitably, dominate the others and deform the other two to itself.

The assertion that one of the three factors will be dominant for a religious person or group is to a large degree a postulate because one cannot survey all religious persons or peoples to determine that it is accurate. But it can be confirmed by exposure to religious persons and groups, and it is helpful for understanding what prevents treating religious people, including adherents of the same religion, as all alike. It allows for anticipating that people even of the same religion can fall into disagreements that are deeply, at times even forcefully, expressed. It provides answers to the question of why and how there are contrasts and even antagonisms not only between religious and nonreligious people and between people of differing religious identities, but also between people of the same religion.

Also, plausibility is granted to this description by the fact that it seems likely or predictable that one of the three factors will dominate the other two. Each of the three carries the potential for becoming or being recognized as deservedly dominant in a religious system. As to the first factor, what cannot be understood or controlled, it makes sense that its form or accessibility in the human world, the second factor, will be less firmly or specifically identifiable, since specific and identifiable access seems to compromise the uncontrollable and mysterious qualities of the first factor. And if emphasis is placed on the second factor, the presence or availability of what cannot be understood or controlled in the human world, this form is taken as shaping and giving content to how the religious person or group should regard what cannot be understood or controlled as well as what are taken to be the human benefits resulting from access to or relations with it. And if attention is given primarily to human well-being, especially what in the world or in persons needs supplementation, correction, or reconstitution, then both the nature of what cannot be understood or controlled and the form of its availability in the human world will be directed toward human well-being, toward countering threats to it, and toward providing necessities and benefits that further it. It is important to recognize, then, that a case can be made to position any of the three components as deserving to be dominant in a religious system.

It is necessary for understanding a religious person or group to recognize, therefore, that all three of these factors are operative, that any one of them can and likely will dominate, and that the dominance of one over the other two factors can be justified and defended. This means that adherents of the same religion can disagree with one another and that people who identify with one religion can understand and even feel some commonality with people from another religion because the others' dominant is similar to their own, more commonality, perhaps, than they feel with people in their own religion whose dominant differs from theirs. It also accounts for the at times violent interactions between adherents of the same religion as well as the aggravating role of this matter for adherents of differing religions and their potentially negative relations to one another. What occurs is that the adherent of one form of a religion sees in another form of the same religion or of another religion the subordinated place and role of what should be dominant, a subordination that is perceived as provocative and even offensive.

It is important to recognize that, while one of the religious-making factors will be for a religious person or people more important than the other two, it is not as though "religious" can be applied to persons or peoples for whom only one of these factors is operative and the other two absent. There are people who are so oriented to and by one of the three factors that they may seem to warrant being referred to as religious. Some may be identified fully with a fascination for what cannot be understood or controlled, others with the occasion or form of accessibility in the human world of that which cannot be understood or controlled, and others with the well-being of other persons or humanity, and this orientation, while carrying beliefs and having a determining role in their lives, may to some degree resemble religious people, but they should not be identified as such. However intense and defining the one factor is for some people, it is not sufficient by itself to identify them as religious. The reason for this is that the three factors that identify a person or people as religious are, while unevenly at play, necessary by their being operative in the process of keeping any one of the three factors from being exclusive.

The conclusion to be drawn from this is that there are three kinds of religious systems that can be or actually are present and determining for religious persons or groups. It would be good if neutral terms were available to designate these three kinds; the terms I use are, unfortunately, more relevant to some religions than to others. But I take some comfort in the fact that Max Weber used similar terms. So, let us call a religious system in which the first factor, the significance and power of what cannot be understood or controlled, is the dominant factor that deforms the other two factors in the system to itself, a *prophetic* system. A system in which the second factor, the location or occasion in the human world that allows what cannot be understood or controlled to be accessed or contacted, is dominant, a *priestly* system. And a religious system in which the third factor, the well-being of the person, group, or humanity made possible by the accessibility in a person's or people's world of what cannot be understood or controlled, dominates the other two can be called, for lack of a better term, a *sapiential* system.

In order to summarize the answer to the question of what we mean when we refer to a person or people as religious, an answer that unifies religious people but also recognizes complexity, difference, and potential conflict, let us exchange the descriptions of the three factors constituting "religious" as listed above for the letters "x," "y," and "z." To illustrate what has been said, then, we have the following:

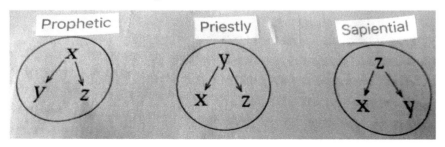

IV

In order to provide these three kinds of religious systems with more clarity and firmness and to anticipate matters that lie ahead, we should see, however briefly, that these three forms can and often will appear in the history of a particular religion, and, since it is the dominant religion in and for Western culture, Christianity is a suitable example. Doing so will also give substance to the suggestion that rifts that arise within a particular religion can be as serious and potentially long-lasting as those that arise between religions. Finally, we should see why conflicts between forms of a single religion and between religions, while certainly aggravated by them, cannot be wholly traced to political and related sources but can also or even more be traced to religion itself and to the relations that the factors making up the differing forms of a religious system have to one another. It is important for Christianity also to say that the three forms of this religion are found not only in its history but also in its scriptures; the Bible contains all three, and advocates of each of the forms can appeal for their case to the authority of biblical texts.

To illustrate the appearance of each of the three forms in the history of Western Christianity, I shall begin with the middle form as previously presented, namely, the one I have called priestly. The dominant of this form, "y," is manifested by the places or occasions that grant human beings access to what cannot be understood or controlled and that are believed to allow for relations between it and those receiving benefits from it. There are reasons why this element of a religious system can be thought obviously deserving of primacy. The first is that the two other elements, "x" and "z," stand to a noticeable extent as contraries to one another. This difference is variously described: eternal and mortal, holy and impure, almighty and fragile, self-sustaining and dependent. The ways of describing this difference, distinction, and even separation are manifold. Indeed, it seems necessary and fruitful for religious persons to be aware of and even to emphasize this difference. Obviously, then, a relation between the two, the human and, let us say, the divine, which would otherwise be contrary to, if not at odds with, one another becomes very important. This relation is made possible by the sites and occasions where and when the two meet or relate to one another. But these places and occasions easily become more than functional mediators or enablers; they have an identity borrowed from both sides, from both the divine and the human.

Defenders of priestly forms will contend against the claims of primacy that lie within or threaten to arise on behalf of "x" or "z." Against making "x" primary, the point that will be made, along with others, is that demoting the primacy of "y" makes human relations with "x" sporadic and unreliable.

Against the case for the primacy of "z," the point will be made, along with others, that human beings ought not to fashion for themselves ways by which relations to "x" are made possible and actualized. The point will further be made that the forms or occasions by which the divine is made accessible or relates to the human reveal in this relation as well as in the distinction between them, what both are, what makes for differences and relations between them. Furthermore, it will likely be affirmed that the places and occasions by which the divine and human can be or are related to one another are, due to the standing of the divine, determined by it, conveying thereby some of its characteristics to them. The conveyance by the divine of some of its characteristics to the place or occasion of its accessibility means that the place or occasion is itself set apart from what is ordinary or contrary to it. This often means that those who administer the location or occasion are themselves also to be set apart by being a particular group conditioned for their important, even unique, role. General participants in the presence or availability made possible by the place or occasion should also highly regard, by means of adequate preparation, what allows them to share in this access and receive its benefits. It is to be expected, then, that priests and other custodians of the places or occasions and participants in them will see themselves receiving their identities and construing their place and time in the world in relation to the occasions and places of divine availability.

The most extensive and firm appearance of a priestly form of Christianity occurred during the so-called high middle ages. Not only for political and other reasons, even though they also played a role, this highly articulated form of Christianity arose because, as already suggested, obvious justifications can be given for the dominance of the "y" element in the system. The dominant presence of the Church and the authority of its clergy were almost definitive of medieval culture, and the beliefs and practices of Christianity were oriented to and given content by ecclesiastical and sacramental beliefs and practices. The Church and its sacraments were not simply the sites and occasions of the accessibility of the divine but were continuous with and affected by the presence of the divine. While the Church took on a centrality that rivaled the standing and role of the Bible, appeals, if necessary, could be made to biblical texts, such as the place and role of sacred sites and occasions, priests, and religious authority in the Hebrew Bible, and to texts warranting the formation of the Church and its importance in the New Testament. We should keep in mind that marks of a "y" factor carrying the potential to become prominent and even dominant can be found in any religion. But its place and role in medieval Christianity is a striking example.

While the so-called Reformation and the rise of Protestantism had many and various sources and antecedents, it arose with remarkable effects in a relatively short period of time. While this can be in part attributed to other cultural and political conditions and the abilities and impact of Reformers as particular persons, the principal cause for it lay in Christianity itself as a religious system. This is because the "x" factor in religious systems, the power and meaning of what cannot be understood or controlled, challenges forms of the religion that emphasize the availability and presence of the divine in the human world. Central to the objection latent in the "x" factor is that the dominance of "y" makes the availability and presence of the divine predicable and confined. This objection will be intensified by the point that those who administer the sites or occasions for that accessibility or presence can come to be seen at least in part as custodians of it. This gives rise to the charge that the divine is made captive to human understandings and controls. Terms like "priest-craft" or idolatry lie in the arsenal of those who advocate for the dominance of "x" in opposition to forms of the religion dominated by "y." Because advocates of a prophetic religious system emphasize the primacy of what cannot be understood or controlled, it is understandable that they will have strongly negative responses to a form of the religion that they perceive as to an objectionable degree claiming to know and control what cannot be understood or controlled.

Prophetic forms of a religion will also take a dim view of sapiential forms. This is because the "x" factor shifts primacy from human potentials and needs to the power and meaningfulness of the divine. Systems dominated by the "x" factor are likely to disparage human abilities and accomplishments, questioning the permanence and positive outcomes of humanly understood and controlled constructions, and will insist that human nature and human needs are primarily revealed by their discontinuous or contrasting standing relative to the divine. Indeed, a contrary relation can develop between those adherents of the religion who emphasize the "x" factor toward those identified with a form in which "z" is dominant. Advocates of prophetic systems likely will also consider human constructions to be marks of or to give rise to human pride and arrogance, to attempts by human beings to take for themselves some characteristics of the primacy that should be ascribed to the divine.

There is no lack of biblical support for advocates of a form of Christianity in which "x" is dominant. The Hebrew prophets were clear about the temptations inherent in human structures and practices, especially those concentrated in the monarchy and the temple, for fostering a false sense of security and of predictable access and relation to the divine. A recurring emphasis among the prophets is on the period in the lives of the people when they wandered in the wilderness and had to depend not on their cities or sacred sites for relations with and benefits from the divine but on the guidance and protection of the divine itself.

Although biblical support was important for the Reformers and for the rise of Protestantism, it should be emphasized that the potential for taking exception in the name of "x" to forms dominated by "y" or "z" lies within the "x" factor itself. When it is underestimated or repressed, when what one could claim as its obvious worthiness for being the dominant is slighted, it can, one could almost say that it will, break out or find spokespersons for it. As is true of all three forms of religion, it is clear that the Reformers in their emphasis on "x" did not exclude or repress the other factors but deformed them toward the dominant. To repeat, it is not possible for a religion that one of the factors in the system should become exclusive. All three are necessary and sufficient, but predictably two of the factors will, to various degrees, be suppressed by and deformed toward the dominant.

The third form of Christianity is one in which the "z" factor is dominant, and the name I give to this form, for lack of a better one, is "sapiential." It is a form of Christianity that makes human needs and potentials dominant, and it is a form that has particular importance in and for Western modernity. The case can and should be made that religion in modernity should not be understood as a diluted, compromised, or essentially humanistic form that robs Christianity of its integrity and force and makes it subservient to secular or nonreligious interests. It is a viable form of Christianity and deserves attention and regard not as attenuated, deficient, or subverted but as having a legitimate and understandable role. The harsh critique of this form of Christianity as a departure or distortion, as potentially or actually secular or humanistic, will arise from those for whom "x" and/or "y" factors are dominant, from those, in other words, who make the "z" factor, which is attentive to human needs and potentials, subservient to and deformed toward either "x" or "y."

Because sapiential forms of Christianity are thought to be compromised or distorted by their focus on human needs and potentials, it may be good to begin by pointing out the biblical bases and warrants for a sapiential religious system. The books of biblical wisdom are the most obvious sources of warrant: Proverbs, Ecclesiastes, Song of Songs, Job, and some of the Psalms. But it should be kept in mind that this form of religion was also identified with the monarchy, and it is important that Solomon stands as a patron and model of wisdom. Another text that could be cited is the remarkable set of Joseph narratives.

Among the many characteristics of biblical wisdom, three stand out. The first and most obvious of them is the attention given to human life as a participant in a created order, or what we think of as nature. The principal manifestation of divine power and meaning in these texts is the created order. Nature is not a passive background but an active participant in human affairs. It is a source of instruction, and it offers, text-like, directives and encourages certain attitudes and behaviors. Humans are placed within the natural context and reminded of its variations, beauties, and force. Life is seen as relational and positive; human lives are continuous with the lives of creatures in their context. The second characteristic or emphasis is on the human as such rather than on particular human beings or a specific people. While particularity or group identity is present, it exists in a human context that includes others. This accounts for its relation to the monarchy, since kings, such as Solomon, had relations, even by marriage, with other peoples. Joseph, while not forgetting his origins and familial relations, turns his positive energies toward the well-being of the people of Egypt and attains a high administrative ranking in its political and economic structure. Indeed, biblical wisdom can be seen as receiving input from other cultures, as is depicted by the exchange of wisdom between Solomon and the Queen of Sheba. The third emphasis is on wisdom itself, which is not the same as knowledge but is also related to it. Wisdom can at least to some degree be taught, albeit not primarily as information or laws but by examples. The pursuit of wisdom has, one could say, a somewhat aesthetic as well as a moral and intellectual aspect. It projects the kind of person one should aspire to be. The pursuit is forward and upward and stands in contrast to foolishness, which is careless, shortsighted, and self-oriented.

Sapiential elements of Christianity can be seen throughout its history, even when subordinated to and deformed by one of the other factors. Regard for nature or the created order, an affirmation of positive relations with people other than oneself or one's group, and the quest for what is worthy or what elevates human life are continuous or recurring emphases. But in the modern period, beginning let us say in the seventeenth century, this form of Christianity begins to come strikingly to the fore and to dominate. This is due in part to political, economic, and cultural developments, especially in explorations of and attention to nature, and to the revived importance of Greek and Roman cultures, but its principal source lies in the "z" element within Christianity itself and its potential of that element to be dominant. Again, this potential is obvious or natural. Religion comes to attention because of its effects on and as a part of human life. Human needs and potentials, well-being, and direction are addressed and abetted by religion shaped by the prominence or dominance of "z." As it is obvious to those advocating one or the other of the two other factors that the dominant in their system deserves that status and force, so also "z" becomes a legitimate and obvious dominant. The lives of people, their world, their relations in and to that world, and their needs and potentials can and should be seen not only as real but as the most important way in which deity and the points of access to it or relations with it are recognized.

Humans are obviously in relations both with other human beings and with the natural context of their lives, and they are to take seriously divine mandates to value and nurture those relations.

Of course, prophetic and priestly advocates will fire back. What they take to be primary and authoritative appears here to be subjected to human needs and potentials, and the eventual dissolving of authoritative accesses to the divine appears as an inevitable outcome. The primacy of "z" will appear to make human beings themselves primary and the other factors subservient to and shaped by human interests. Indeed, a sapiential religious system can become so determined by attention to human needs and potentials that it begins no longer to be a religious system, but this is the case with the other constituents, "x" and "y," as well. When those who speak in advocacy of either "x" or "y" factors so that it becomes not prominent or even dominant but exclusive, it destroys the system as religious. Sapiential forms, like the others, become less religious as the other characteristics are slighted or ignored. As violence is a recurring threat to the viability of prophetic systems and as exclusivity and authoritarianism are threats to the health of a priestly system, so also materialism, secularism, and humanism are threats to sapiential religious systems.

Indeed, it can be argued that emphasis on human needs and potentials and on human well-being do become exclusive in late modernity. The objections of spokespersons for a sapiential system to the obstructive and repressive effects on human well-being of prophetic and priestly systems can give rise to rejecting altogether the place and role of "x" and 'y" factors in a religious system, leaving the human as the exclusive point of attention and leaving "z" to stand alone as defining the nature and role of what is taken to be religious but no longer is.

A person or group can be called religious, then, only if all three factors constituting a religious system are detectable. One of the three will be dominant for any particular religious person or group, but the subordinated factors must continue to be operative. When the dominance of one of the factors becomes so pronounced as to virtually overshadow the place and role of either or both of the other two, distortions arise, and the viability and integrity of the religion are threatened.

It is hoped that this proposal concerning what is meant by referring to some persons or peoples as religious is sufficiently clear to be understandable and applicable while also complex and flexible enough to cover a wide range of differences between religious and nonreligious people, between people of differing religious identities, and between people of the same religion. It is important for understanding religion to see that the potential for variety, difference, and even conflict within and between religions is due, as is also the cause for the rise of a religion or the reason for being religious, not necessarily to something nonreligious. However, it is also the case that religion is related to much else that is part of human lives and cultures. The religion of a person, group, or culture is always embedded in and affected by its situation. Personal and psychological, social and political, and cultural and natural elements inevitably are involved, but these factors in a religion, while always there, should not be taken as necessarily primary or causative. Being religious involves relations with many other things, but being religious is also distinguishable from them.

Chapter 6

THE POSITION OF THE PERSON STUDYING RELIGION

We turn now from the object of religious studies, from the question of what is being studied, namely, religious people, to questions concerning the person studying religion and the position taken toward religion by the person studying it. This is a question as important, elusive, and complex for the study of religion as the previous one. While it is a factor relevant to any study, the position of the person studying religion is particularly important because, as already suggested, it can be expected that persons will have sharply differing opinions as to the understanding and evaluation of religion that will affect the stance taken toward religion while studying it. These differences also affect the relations to one another of people who study religion because there are extremes that are not only theoretically possible but also actively taken that are firm and conflict with one another. On one side are people identifiable as believing that there is only one religion, their own, and that all others should either be discredited or ignored. On the other side are people who believe that religion is objectionable and is based on mistaken or fanciful assumptions and ideas, on the desire of some people to elevate themselves above others, or on the need to conceal or justify what is actually most important to them, namely, power or privilege.

This question also comes to the fore because of the two differing sources upon which departments of religious studies drew and by which they continue to be affected. One, as we have seen, is the history of religious studies that was and continues to be a part of academic culture, particularly the social sciences. This source, while not homogeneous, was unified in its not being sponsored by scholars whose work was shaped primarily by their own religious identities and concerns but rather by an interest in human nature and cultures. Attention was directed toward religion because of the obvious role played by it in the lives of people and in the cultures studied. However, it is also clear that the scholars at whom we looked had their own opinions or beliefs concerning the continuing roles and standing of religion in modernity.

Meanwhile, as we saw, departments of religious studies in the decades immediately following the Second World War were founded or augmented by faculty largely drawn from graduate programs in religious studies located in institutions religiously identifiable, particularly with Protestant Christianity. While usually also trained in scholarly methods and interests found in other departments, such as the social sciences, especially historical studies, it could be assumed that their orientations were primarily based on and shaped by their own religious identities and interests. Since the administrations of institutions inaugurating or expanding departments of religious studies left to the new or expanded faculties the task of shaping the departmental curriculum, it is not surprising that the resulting curricula primarily matched those of theological studies in Protestant institutions, particularly biblical studies, the history of Christianity, and Christian theology and ethics.

These two sources for the formation of religious studies were to some degree compatible. As we have seen, the already existing forms of religious studies in other departments, especially in the social sciences, gave close, extensive, and often appreciative attention to the role and standing of religion in the lives of people and cultures that they studied. Correspondingly, faculty who formed or expanded departments of religious studies in the decades following the Second World War were also trained in graduate programs influenced by academic methods and interests in both the social sciences and the humanities. This often resulted in faculty who, while primarily identified with and focused on Christianity, were also able to pursue their work in relation to methods and findings of scholarship in other departments. However, despite factors that eased the differences between the religiously and nonreligiously motivated and oriented scholars studying religion, the difference between them remained recognizable and continues now.

As we turn to address some of the consequences for the study of religion caused by noticeable differences between scholars more identifiable with one or with the other of the two sides, we should do so with some urgency because the present situation of detectable or felt difference and even tension between the two sides weakens the standing and role of religious studies. This is because the study of religion could be taken from its present departmental locations and returned to the two contrary and formative sources from which they are derived: locations in other departments for the nonreligious study of religion and, on the other hand, locations for the religious study of religion in religiously identifiable situations on or off the campus. In addition, it should be kept in mind that the extreme positions available concerning this matter continue to have influence. One does not need to go far to find those for whom religion should not be seen as in itself worthy of study but of being reduced to something else or discredited as illusion and wishful thinking, and those who assume that only one religion is worthy of study while others are seen to be mistaken or objectionable. When it is proposed, as I shall, that the person studying religion should be conscious of and also honest about his or her position regarding this difference, there are considerations that make this self-positioning difficult. Present conditions seem to encourage reticence, and that seems to be the prevailing practice. But the uncertainty that reticence creates conceals the threat of the difference to religious studies as a coherent academic field. An attempt should be made to identify a basis upon which mutuality between these two approaches toward the study of religion can be recognized and put forward.

I

For reasons already given, people studying religion will vary depending on which of the three religion-making characteristics they think is or should be more important than the other two. It is useful, while studying religion, to determine what the dominant element is in each case and how it shapes the religious material being studied, but it is also important for those studying religion to be aware of what their own position is relative to the three possibilities. This is important because of the tendency not only to see one of the elements of religion as dominant relative to the others but also to assume that this choice is obviously the right one.

Another important matter concerning the position of the person studying religion is the prominence and eventual dominance in the formation of Western modernity, including academic culture, of what I have called "sapiential" religious forms. I ventured to propose that the primary and enabling context for the rise of religious studies as we know it today was provided to a noticeable degree by Romanticism. While it is unlikely that a conscious intention of the scholars to whom earlier we turned was to advance a Romantic agenda and while it would not do to call Romanticism a religious movement, it was a movement in reaction to major characteristics of modernity and supportive of an interest in differing kinds of people, cultures, and human experiences, particularly those other than and even counter to the increasingly clear direction of Western modernity. These scholars, while differing from one another, shared an interest in and concern for human needs, potentials, and well-being that they thought were neglected when the dominant focus of modernity concentrates on advancements in understanding and control taken as materially determined. This noticeable concern for their own culture, for modernity, that is detectable in the work of the scholars at whom we looked is consonant with the major components or emphases of Romanticism. Both religious studies and Romanticism were directed toward an expanded and deepened awareness and appreciation of human nature. It could be said that Romanticism helped to turn religious interests toward the human, and religious studies helped to turn human interests toward religion. Both drew attention to, among other things, what is not determined by human rationality and control and is not causally traceable to material.

We also saw that the remarkable rise of academic interest in the study of religion after the Second World War created the need for faculty in religious studies and that they were drawn in large part from graduate programs in religion located in institutions with religious identities. However, these identities were housed less in institutions with strong and specific religious identities and more in those with more general or diverse relations to religion. It is fair to say that the institutions from which faculty to fill newly created positions in departments of religious studies were institutions that related the study of religion to broader academic and cultural interests. To refer to the previous chapter, we could say that the faculty that came to fill the newly created or expanded departments were identified with and drawn from academic religious contexts that could be called sapiential rather than priestly or prophetic. The interests in religion that motivated and directed the rise and continued development of religious studies, then, were directed primarily toward the place and role of religion in relation to human needs, potentials, and well-being. Meanwhile, the scholars at whom we looked in the first part of this book were also, as we shall see, aware of the other two constitutive elements of religion, but their work was shaped primarily by a preoccupation with human potentials and needs. This is not to fault either the interests we traced in the first part of this book or those of scholars who filled the rather rapid founding or expanding of departments of religious studies in the middle of the twentieth century. Rather, it means that the study of religion as we now know it was deeply affected, if not determined, by sapiential religious assumptions and values, and they continue to be so.

In Chapter 5, I questioned Jonathan Z. Smith's caveats concerning the meanings or references of the terms "religion" and "religious," his conclusion that the interests brought to the study of religion determine the meaning or references of the terms and not something residing in that to which the study of religion directs attention. He questioned the putative standing or even usefulness of the terms because of the varying ways in which they are used. I responded by saying, that despite variation, there is a steadiness in the uses of these terms that gives them a standing and role. But when we take into account that to which we now turn, namely, to what those who study religion bring to the task, his point gains weight. Indeed, we can conclude that the study of religion is also affected by assumptions and convictions about religion that those who study it bring with them. Religious studies as we know it today depends primarily on an interest in religion and an approach to the study of it that takes as primary and even dominant not factors of an "x" or "y" sort, of what I called a prophetic or priestly kind, but factors of a "z" kind, that is, of religion understood as it relates to human needs, potentials, and well-being. When we look at religious studies today, we can see not only a measure of agreement about the standing and role of religion in the lives of people and cultures but also a difference that arises among scholars concerning religion's value or role in human lives. For the most part, religious studies was directed not only by people identifiable with sapiential forms of religion but also by people who understood religion as having positive roles in human lives and cultures. A major question, one that has come increasingly to the fore, concerns the relation of religion to human well-being. Answers to this question are important indicators of the relation of the person studying religion to what is being studied.

There are three kinds of responses to the question of whether religion has a negative or positive relation to human well-being. One of them is that religion, however various in nature and role and however subject to change over time, is a continuing and, let us say, natural part of human life. Human beings are, in this view, inherently religious. Understanding human beings and cultures, even those of today, therefore, requires inclusion of religious studies. There always have been and there will continue to be people who are identifiable as religious, and this is because religion is a part of how people, either individually or in groups, are constituted. A second option or assumption is that religion gave most people in the past and continues to give some people in the present matters important to their lives, but religion's role in human lives and cultures need not any longer be continued but can either be brushed aside as something personal and even idiosyncratic or replaced by something nonreligious that in some manner or to some extent plays roles once played by religion. The third option is that religion, however important it was and continues to be for some people and however interesting it may be to study, is not only outmoded but is mistaken and even, potentially or actually, harmful to human life and well-being. While some scholars self-identify with one or another of these three options, the position taken is usually not declared, however much it should be.

Two things are important to see in these three options. The first is that they are not confined to scholarly circles but find support in the culture because religion has been or continues to be personally and culturally active and needs to be taken into account and evaluated. Religion continues to be a sufficiently major, recurring, or enduring aspect of human lives, societies, and cultures to deserve attention and to require a judgment regarding its standing and role, especially in relation to human well-being. People who study religion can assume that religion is not something insubstantial, private, or peripheral but enters and influences a wide variety of contemporary cultural, social, political, and economic arenas. Studying religion implies, even requires, taking it seriously. While those who study religion will encounter academic colleagues who think of religion as inconsequential or irrelevant, a matter solely of personal whim or taste, it is important for persons studying religion, even if they regard it as harmful to human well-being, to defend the estimation of religion as a major factor in human lives and cultures that deserves attention. Implied by this question is the question of whether or not, if religion is regarded as outgrown or as harmful, it can or should be replaced by something else. Can human needs and potentials be adequately and positively addressed nonreligiously?

In considering the question of the current standing of religious studies, attention should be given to the fact that the work of scholars reviewed earlier who were located primarily in the social sciences and those referred to as coming into newly founded or expanded departments from religiously identifiable locations, especially Protestant, reveals that religion should be regarded not only as a significant part of human lives and cultures in the past or distant places but also, in varying degrees, as relevant to understanding and evaluating modern culture. As we saw, these scholars tend to relate their interests in religion to their awareness of lacks that appear in their own culture, and they appear to relate those lacks to the reduced roles played by religion in modern culture. The reduction of religion's cultural role in modernity, it is suggested or implied, creates particular lacks for human well-being that need to be addressed. Interest in and concern for their own culture is a part of and in varying degrees a concern affecting their studies. Implied is an argument supporting the study of religion, namely, that religion makes important contributions to personal and communal well-being and that, if it no longer plays those roles, substitutes should be found that will fill the lacks left by religion's retreat. The question arises concerning the relation of those substitutes to human needs, potentials, and well-being. Religious studies today largely retains the assumption that religion is integral rather than exotic or incidental in and for human lives and cultures and that, if religion is deemed no longer relevant to human needs and potentials, something else will, it appears necessarily, take its place and play similar roles. The conclusion to be drawn from this is that the study of religion has cultural and academic significance and urgency. The study of religion explores and exposes the mutuality or reciprocity between religion and human lives and cultures, and this mutuality or reciprocity is true not only for the relations between religion and the lives and cultures of earlier or other peoples but also between religion and the denizens of modern Western culture.

The question of the value of religion and, consequently, also of religious studies, is presently complicated by two contrary developments, both of which are threats to the standing and role of religious studies. One of them sees religion as self-contained and, while involved with culture, separable and basically isolated from and even contrary to it. Culture, in this view, is occasional and of secondary importance relative to religion and has more often than not a diverting and even distorting effect on it. In this view, the study of religion should treat religion as independent of or as only secondarily or incidentally related to personal and cultural concerns. It is not the case, for this view, that human interests and concerns should be called on to judge the value of religion in relation to human needs, potentials, and well-being. The second view, contrary to the first, is that the study of religion is peripheral or even irrelevant and obstructive to cultural studies as presently carried on because religion has no standing or role of its own but is a substitute for or symptom of something else that is causal to it, something nonreligious, secular, or, as is usually the case, material. The role and standing of religious studies are threatened by both of these positions and their contrary relations to one another. The judgment prosecuted by this guide to religious studies is that both of these contrary views of the place and role of religion relative to human needs, potentials, and well-being are partial and need as much as possible to be related to one another.

The first of them, namely, that religion, even though a constant in human lives and cultures, needs to be viewed apart from them so that religion's independence from and primacy relative to culture are secured. Religion is taken, on this view, to have an identity and integrity derived not from human needs and potentials but from a cause apart from or transcendent to them. It is this aspect of religion that needs, for this opinion, to be primary. While cultural entanglements occur, they can be separated from the religion studied and viewed as secondary and even negative relative to it. Having seen the complexity of religious systems in the previous chapter, we can see that this position can be expected to appear mostly from those who view religion from a position dominated more by priestly and/or prophetic than by sapiential factors. What is required in response to this position is to stake out a place for taking sapiential aspects and forms of religion as potentially being as much a part of a religious tradition as are its priestly and/or prophetic forms. Short of this, they need to recognize that a religion is always shaped or influenced by the culture and human lives in which it is operative. This position, that a religion can and should be disentangled from the cultures in which it is involved, seems based on the fact that some religions extend geographically and historically over several cultures, and this may give rise to the assumption that the religion is itself constant and unified while it also attaches to, absorbs, and is compromised by various cultural forms. It is assumed that a religion has an identity or continuity that transcends particular and various cultures in which it is variously implicated. However, what needs to be emphasized in response to this position is that religion is necessarily embedded culturally and is always affected, positively or negatively, by its cultural setting. The relations of religion and culture to one another takes the form of mutual indebtedness.

On the other, contrary, side, religious studies is threatened by the view that human cultures need to be studied in their primacy to and independence from religion. Religion, if given attention, is taken as culturally caused or as concealing something nonreligious that is more basic. For reasons already given, this assumption about religion's secondary, derivative, or unnecessary position relative to culture, while it takes various forms and expressions, finds its firmest base today, whether recognized or not, in practical or theoretical materialism.

The increasingly shared and determining presence of practical and theoretical materialism in academic culture has had results for the study of religion. One sign of this is the increased shaping of religious studies by a primary interest in what is often now called "material religion," that is, for example, the artifacts, statistical accounts of religious organizations and affiliations, or the behaviors and attitudes of religious people. While the shift in focus to the material in religious studies serves as a needed corrective to the prominence and even dominance in religious studies of Protestantism's emphasis on texts, doctrines, and beliefs, this shift also has the perceivable effect of relating departments of religious studies too strongly to departments in the social sciences. However, the consequence of this move, if not restrained, leads to a reduction of religious studies to its material aspects and, even further, to an account of religion as determined by material causes, functions, and consequences.

There are, then, two contrary threats to the integrity of religious studies, the one that treats religion, let us say, idealistically as an essence that can be separated or abstracted from its cultural settings, and the other that treats religion as materialistically caused and sponsored. While both sides, idealist and materialist, should be resisted, studying religion must also retain relations with both. Religious studies must establish its place by relating but not capitulating either to religiously determined or to materialistic methods and theories. Doing this requires first of all a recognition that religious studies is and should be based on the form of religion dominant in modernity, namely, a sapiential form, and that this form has relations on the one side to prophetic and priestly forms and on the other side to human and cultural needs, potentials, and well-being.

II

The question now arises as to whether religious studies, by treating religion in relation to human needs, potentials, and well-being, can retain room for and even interest in the prophetic and priestly aspects of religion. Or is it necessary that a student of religion must, if that person retains a religious identity, adopt one that is dominantly or entirely sapiential? We can address this question by returning briefly to the history of religious scholarship at which we looked in the first part of this book to see how the relations between what is dominant for them, namely, the sapiential factor, and the other two religion-making characteristics are negotiated.

It is possible to say that the work of five theorists and researchers at which we looked under the heading of retrieving what the culture of human advancement has neglected or repressed reveals some dependence on the "prophetic" element in religion. That is, it assumes or suggests that humans in their preoccupation with what they can understand, construct, and control tend to neglect or repress the value of what cannot be understood or controlled because it lies outside their preoccupations. Those in the first group make what is neglected or repressed vital and significant, often causative, relative to what is projected or constructed as understandable and controllable. But, while giving some attention to prophetic elements in religion, the emphasis in these examples remains on human needs and potentials. We should briefly describe this dynamic in their work.

Bachofen sets up a contrary relation between earlier matriarchal societies and the patriarchal formations that arise from, but then neglect or suppress, them. Patriarchal societies are oriented primarily to advancement and the history of achievements at the expense of neglecting what is provided to and not created or secured by them. He implies that a cultural suppression occurs by which what is primary for humans and upon which they depend, such as birth, nurture, meaningful wholeness, the primacy of life over achievement, of unity and relations over distinctions, and of caring for the vulnerable over power, are overridden by what is derivative and secondary. His prophetic point, however, does not call for a reestablishment of matriarchy; it is at most a corrective to excesses that occur in a culture overly determined by human advancements in understanding and control. He calls for more awareness and appreciation of human or natural matters and resources that patriarchal societies tend to neglect and repress.

Something of this kind can also be said of Müller's work. The human capacity for the Infinite and his argument that it precedes the identification of the Infinite with celestial bodies is a prophetic emphasis. The role of natural objects for specifying the Infinite is necessary or understandable but secondary and derivative, and it needs to be seen as dependent on an initial awareness of the Infinite. His prophetic point is that something that cannot be controlled or understood is primary to what can be, but the emphasis falls not as much on the Infinite itself as on the human capacity to be made conscious of it. He also shifts his emphasis to the presence and roles of religion in human life and history, made possible especially by texts and an understanding of them.

Frazer, by relating early religion to desire and violence, implies the prophetic point that cultures develop from what precedes them, namely, vitality, spontaneity, and disruption. However, cultural advance is traced by the taming of these more disruptive elements or forces. For Frazer, the role of religion in human culture is more a matter of the past than of the present; but the effect of his work is also to provide a way for contemporary readers who are not themselves religious to have an appreciation of religion as accounting for resources from which humans can draw. His study of religion implies attention, then, to something empowering and reinvigorating, but also threatening, that a culture of construction and security tends to forget or repress.

A prophetic ingredient is more recognizable in Jung's contributions to religious studies, primarily the sustaining, unifying, and renewing resources of human life underlying knowledge and agency in the unconscious realm that is made available, among other ways, in religious myths, symbols, and patterns. By positing the archetypes of the collective unconscious not only as available in religion but also as affecting culture and human well-being in general, he gives primacy to human potentials that are deep and often contrary to the effects on persons of a culture of knowledge and control. The value of these underlying resources is their vitalizing and unifying effects on persons and cultures. However, these resources, while designated as beyond human understanding and control, are also humanly located.

Turner's focus on the liminal stage in the ritual process is a prophetic emphasis because it brings a society from the structured back to the unstructured, from the realized back to the potential, from distinctions back to commonality, and from the derivative back to the primary. His emphasis on the standing and effects of liminality and on ritual as the means of accessing it gives his work a noticeable prophetic emphasis, which also becomes clear when he calls attention to the roles of the liminal in modern Western forms, such as monastic life, marginalized and excluded people, the work of artists who take exception or provide alternatives to prevailing social interests, and the roles of the poor and weak. A prophetic emphasis defers to the human need and potential to acknowledge and more fully to trust what is important for personal and cultural well-being, namely, the resources that lie prior to, behind, or beneath social structures and to which rituals grant access. Like the others in this group, Turner understands and presents religion in a way that calls attention to prophetic interests, but, like them, too, he retains the sapiential factor as dominant.

Turning now to the second set of interests, we find a detectable awareness of what in religion I have called "priestly" factors. However, as in the previous group, the sapiential factor is dominant in their understandings of religion.

Herbert Spencer is primarily concerned with how societies establish and maintain themselves as collectives, and he places religion in the role of providing what is needed, namely, a response to threats. In early religions, the principal threat is death, and a response to this threat is an emphasis on the value of the community and its survival. The realm of the dead eventually becomes less of a threat and more of a protector because the realm of the dead is transcendent. Spencer includes a priestly factor by identifying access to the transcendent by means of rituals, but the dominant factor remains sapientitial because he grounds the socially unifying effect of religion in the experience of people being brought together in the face of a common threat, as in war or natural catastrophe.

For William James, what people need and what religion can and does provide is delivery from alienation or loneliness by means of feeling at home not only or first of all in society but in the universe. This feeling of ontological inclusion is for him basic to psychological health. It is provided in experiences that are accessed by means of the unconscious and that can, in a general way, be described as experiences of the "more." While the "more" exposes a prophetic element in his understanding of religion, a priestly element is suggested by the role of the unconscious in accessing it. Some people by nature or nurture already feel at home in the universe, but there are others, people to whom James is particularly attentive, who need an exchange of alienation for a sense of relation and inclusion. Religion has a priestly effect in relating persons in their alienation to a wider reality by which they can be secured. However, the capacity for an exchange of alienation and insecurity for inclusion and mutuality is humanly located and retains, thereby, the dominance of the sapiential factor.

Emil Durkheim, like Spencer, turns attention to social inclusion and identity. His background and cultural setting made him familiar with group identity and the rituals that create or maintain a sense of belonging. While there are nonreligious ways of increasing group identity, he distinguishes religious from nonreligious ways by the contrast of the sacred to the profane. The sacred and his identifying the totem as the primary way by which communal identity is secured expose priestly elements, but he does so primarily by describing their roles and standings in relation to human needs, potentials, and well-being. While religiously inspired experiences of mutuality are recognizable as distinguishable and valuable in human life, they are also accounted for by Durkheim as causally identified with human capacities.

For Max Weber, religion also grants something intangible that in any case is necessary for human lives, namely, a sense of motivation and direction. Acting meaningfully and having goals are often conveyed to people by the effects on them of charismatic figures. In this and in other ways, Weber's theory of religion includes priestly elements because religion gives people access to what is more important and meaningful than they themselves are, to what gives their lives motivation, meaning, and direction. However, people's need and capacity to be meaningfully motivated and directed are for him humanly located.

For Robert Bellah, religion can be identified with the human need and potential for a realm that stands as distinguishable from ordinary life. He sees the role of such a realm already in animal behaviors where an arena of play provides acceptance, trust, and care. Arising from maternal nurturing, by which the gift of unconditional support is embodied, safe play provides a departure from life's stresses and access to a realm of affirmation and renewal. People need access to a realm free from self-preoccupation and related to social or human commonality. In recent American culture, Bellah suggests, religion has become a matter primarily of personal choice, resulting in a decline in regard for collective identity and for an interest in the common good. Provision of and access to a realm apart, its reality and alternative roles, posits a priestly factor to his theory of religion, a realm that nurtures what he calls "habits of the heart." However, this need and potential is humanly or naturally located, identifying Bellah's theory as sapiential.

All of these theorists, while including prophetic and priestly ingredients in their accounts of religion, defer to the sapiential factor. However, those in the third group are more fully attentive to the third religion-making characteristic, namely, benefits to human life that result from religion. Part of the reason for this is that providing a worldview, an understanding primarily personal but also communal, of the wider world of which a person or group is a part is central to individual and corporate human identities. For these scholars, the principal benefit provided to people by religion is a comprehensive understanding of their world and of their places within and their relations to it.

E. B. Tylor calls attention to religion's contribution to worldviews by suggesting that we find religion in human cultures no matter how distant or different from our own they may be because religion enables people to have a comprehensive understanding of themselves and their world that delivers them from fragmentation and uncertainty. Religious worldviews are inclusive by affirming the reality of the spiritual in addition to the material and the relation of the two to one another. Religion, then, has been and for many continues to be a beneficial resource from which people draw to form adequate worldviews. Tylor's treatment of a spiritual reality separable for religious people from material has a noticeably transcendent reference, and its role in the formation of an adequate worldview for modern culture is, for him, waning, thereby identifying the capacity for the spiritual as culturally dependent.

Sigmund Freud is more pointed in his assessment of the importance for worldviews of religion's contributions to them. The need for worldviews continues, but, more explicitly than Tylor, he holds out scientifically and rationally informed worldviews as replacements for those with religious ingredients and supports. While people continue to need a worldview, they should outgrow religious orientations and explanations and rely on rationally and empirically verifiable understandings. He recognizes, however, that rational and empirical accounts of the world are presently not able to provide the adequate worldview that people need. Unlike Tylor, who implies the continuing role in modernity at least of religious vestiges, Freud wants to dissolve dependence on or use of religion altogether. For him it is better, while we wait, to carry on as well as possible with an inadequate worldview than to have one that includes what he considers to be wishful thinking or illusion.

What is unusual in Malinowski's work is his contention that early societies did not have worldviews constructed entirely in religious ways. Early societies were able to distinguish between empirically or rationally and religiously formed understandings and practices. Moderns tend to think that the distinction in their own culture between science or technology and religion is unique, but Malinowski was able to establish that early societies had worldviews that distinguished between the two kinds of practices and understandings. He implies that the worldviews of early societies, although complex, were coherent because of the unifying compass of religion, particularly through the effects of the totem. He also suggests that magic played a mediating cultural role between science or technology and religion. Finally, Malinowski contends that the profane in early or traditional societies does not have the negative and contrary force that some scholars of religion attribute to it. The profane is or can be less of a threat and more of a neutral potential.

A major implication of Eliade's work is that religiously constructed worldviews persist, however attenuated, in modern cultures. He bases this claim on what he takes to be basic for a religiously informed worldview, namely, that it offers adherents a coherent whole by orienting them meaningfully both temporally and spatially. This is done by the role for temporality of beginnings or origins and for spatiality of the center. Primarily in relation to natural cycles, ordinary time is made meaningful by being restored to the primordial time of beginnings. Spatially, religion orients people to the center of the world in relation to which other places are peripheral. These resources in traditional religions are weakened in modernity by a displacement of cyclical by linear or historical time and an underestimation of the effects of the profane. However, while the profane, which is contrary to the sacred, has had negative impacts on modern Western understandings, a sense of and desire for the sacred remains, evinced by the rituals and affirmations that relate people, although often in individual and improvised ways, to beginnings and to centers.

Clifford Geertz is even more explicit about the relevance of religion to an adequate worldview. Religion, while closely related to culture, is of the two the more comprehensive and stable. It relates metaphysical, physical, and ethical matters to one another and to daily activities and challenges. For Geertz, being human requires a worldview that allows a person or people to have meaningful relations in and to their world. A worldview need not be a complete set of interlocking understandings; it needs only to be sufficiently adequate that when things are encountered or occur that are dissonant relative to a worldview assurance can be retained that somehow or at some later time dissonance will be at least to some degree resolved. Like others among these examples, Geertz implies that a major lack in modern Western culture is a shared, comprehensive, and coherent worldview stabilized by religious beliefs and practices. Like the others in this group as well as the examples of theorists in the other two categories, he understands religion in relation to the human needs and potentials that religion addresses and provides by positing sapiential factors as dominant.

These theorists, while making sapiential factors in religion dominant, recognize and include detectable prophetic and priestly elements. This is to say, they treat religion as a religion even though they do not give prominent, and still less dominant, places to religious elements other than sapiential. They also retain, in their attention to religion as related to human needs, potentials, and well-being, understandings of religion that indicate the presence, although often peripheral, of the other two factors necessary to referring to human lives and cultures as recognizably religious. They agree that people have been, and to some degree continue to be, religious because religion substantially contributes to their personal and communal lives and well-being.

III

The point that religious studies as we know it favors and is even shaped by one and not all three forms that religion can take, that is, by a sapiential understanding of religion, helps to clarify its present academic placement and role.

If studying religion continues to be a form of academic interest, it will do so primarily in its attention to human needs, potentials, and well-being, to lacks in the current culture, and to ways by which religion can and in various ways does address these lacks. It follows that academic culture can, without itself being religious, include and support kinds of academic interests identifiable as sapientially religious. It also follows that religious studies, described as it here has been, opens the way for current scholars in religious studies to relate both to alternative religious approaches to the study of religion, particularly in prophetic or priestly religious forms, and to colleagues in other, particularly social science, departments. Indeed, secular academic institutions can support religious studies without becoming religiously identified, while at the same time countering the trend in academic culture to discount or dismiss needs and potentials in human life and culture not adequately treated by accounts that rest finally on materialistic assumptions and beliefs.

While there may be other sources on which to draw for making the case that religious studies can establish and maintain its academic standing and role and at the same time retain its regard for religious beliefs and practices and their relevance to human life and culture, two sources have been referred to in this guide and should be noted more specifically. The first of them lies in the continuing and necessary role in contemporary culture of nonreligiously based beliefs. As already indicated, it can be argued that human well-being, both personal and cultural, cannot be adequately advanced and supported by attitudes, behaviors, and positions based only or even primarily on material or rational warrants. Beliefs are required, and they continue to operate within the culture, including the academy. Regard for other people, for future generations, for those with whom one differs or who are by others dismissed or exploited, and for the natural environment has been and can be religiously based, but it is not wholly dependent on religious support. The presence and effects of these beliefs in an increasingly nonreligious culture may well be due to their being survivals or vestiges of a previous and more religiously informed culture. But nonreligious moral directives and sensitivities, along with generous and compassionate people, are obviously important. Appeals and relations to them can extend religious studies in a positive direction toward this basis for wider support. These relations can begin with such identifiable and growing numbers of people who self-identify as "spiritual but not religious" people, those, in other words, who recognize the limitations and potential negative consequences of goals and values based entirely on materialist bases or on self and group identities.

A second resource is the continuing and still meaningful relation of contemporary culture to Romanticism, with which the rise of religious studies as we now know it can be associated. While Romanticism was not itself primarily religious and was a culturally diverse movement or climate, it carried within itself religious interests and formed a response to the rapid changes in human life wrought by material determinants such as urbanization, industrialization, and technological achievements. Romanticism and religious studies shared and gave mutual support to one another, specifically their common orientation to and by human needs and potentials that the emerging culture seemed unprepared adequately to appreciate or to address.

Attention both to nonreligious beliefs in the culture and to the continuing effects of Romanticism can serve to strengthen the case for religious studies as having both a diagnostic and an ameliorating relation to academic and general culture. Both turn interests in human and cultural studies toward religion and religious societies and away from dependence on the putative sufficiency of materialistically shaped methods and goals.

Implied by my examples of the interests taken by the emergence of religious studies is the conclusion that those who study religion can and should have a more secure place than they now have between contrary interests on both sides of it. These two contrary sides, as already indicated, are, on the one side, an explicit religious position that tends to subject human needs, potentials, and well-being to its own terms and, on the other side, materialist methods and assumptions that tend to reduce human life and culture to terms rationally and empirically certain. At a minimum, the interests in religion that should be brought by those working in religious studies should be marked primarily by an emphasis on the continuing standing and role of religion in relation to human needs, potentials, and well-being. This emphasis should include those that are historically traceable by the examples of religious scholarship that have been described: 1) a recognition of and renewed appreciation for the sources and resources that lie in what is neglected and underappreciated when a culture is preoccupied with construction, advancement, and control; 2) the accesses provided by religion to intangible realities, both personal and cultural, that address human needs exposed by the determining effects of late modernity, such as dislocation, individualism, and a loss of meaningful goals; 3) and the need for adequate and sustaining worldviews, especially worldviews that relate the material in human life to elevating, just, and edifying values and norms Each of these three interests is sufficiently wide, elastic, and complex enough to warrant their continuing academic and cultural relevance and their openness to additional interests of many kinds.

To return, in conclusion, to the question raised and addressed by this chapter, namely, the position of the person studying religion in the context of religious studies, we can say that that position is complex, but it is so in a healthy way. It does not have the certainty that is enjoyed by the options on either side of it, namely, the certainty and adequacy of religious identity and accounts and the certainty of human sciences dependent on methods drawn from an academic culture increasingly determined by materialist methods and interests. The position of those studying religion in the context of religious studies does not have, like most positions taken between sharply divided contraries, fixity and unity. It even, like other positions of its kind, lacks a name. It is primarily diagnostic and remedial in its methods and interests, testing for personal and cultural faults and deficiencies, and turning to religion as a resource from which to draw for exposing and redressing them.

Chapter 7

TAKING INTO ACCOUNT RELIGION'S EXCESSES AND COMPLEXITIES

Having addressed two major areas of uncertainty, the first more objective, namely, how to identify what it is that one studies in religious studies, and the second more subjective, namely, the various attitudes toward or interests in religion that the student of it can bring to the task, we turn now to difficulties and excesses in religion that complicate the study of it and are difficult to avoid or resolve. While the treatment of the previous topics, religion itself and the person studying it, was mostly positive, a tone consistent with the quite positive treatment of religion's relation to human needs and potentials in the first part of this book, a treatment implying a more negative evaluation of modernity than of religion, we must now shift to viewing religion more negatively.

This turn is necessary because the student of religion will encounter some form of critique or objection to religion accusing it of being damaging in its effects on personal, social, and cultural well-being. The principal point to be made is that these objections are not without merit because religion carries within it causes and bases for excesses and distortions. Three factors give rise to roles taken by religion that are questionable and even objectionable, roles that account at least in part for critiques of religion that go so far as to consider it to be not a resource for addressing human needs and potentials but a bane for personal, social, and cultural well-being. We shall consider three characteristics or complexities of religion that carry potentials that cause or contribute to its having questionable and even objectionable standings in and consequences for human lives and cultures.

I

The first and perhaps most common cause of tensions and excesses in religion is anticipated by the definition of religious people that I offered and that is basic to this guide. I defined religious people as exhibiting three distinguishable characteristics, an awareness of and orientation toward what cannot be understood or controlled, the availability in the human world of access to or relations with what cannot be understood or controlled, and the beneficial consequences for human well-being of relations with what cannot be understood or controlled. I then proposed that all three of these components need to be present if we are to identify a person or group as religious, but I also proposed that each of the three constitutive elements carries within it potentials for being dominant in relation to the other two, for subjecting the two other components, and for deforming the other two toward itself. While religions share a skeletal set of religion-making characteristics, they also carry potentials for disagreement, tension, and even conflict both between and within religions. By its very constitution religion carries potentials to take on differing and even conflicting forms created by one or another of its components exercising dominance over the other two. A factor that intensifies this complexity and instability is that people can see what they themselves consider to be the rightful dominant placed in a subordinate position by others for whom a differing element is and should be dominant. This readily results in the defenders' rising to the cause of asserting the rightful dominance of the element they see as repressed and deformed. This will understandably be met with resistance by those convinced that a different element should be dominant.

Aggravating the potential for conflict that resides within religion itself is that when conflicts arise they are often not solely contained within religious interests but have other interests tied to or carried by them. It is important, when recognizing that other interests aggravate religious differences and conflicts, not to err by treating religious conflicts as actually reducible to nonreligious factors, such as cultural, political, or economic interests. Religious conflicts will include interests that are nonreligious because religious people and groups are also identified with and by cultural, political, and economic factors not only attached to their religion but also interpreted and justified by it. Even more, a person's or people's religion is embedded in and affected by aspects drawn into it from its context. Because the potential for conflict lies both within religion itself and its context, it is important, when examining religious conflicts, to recognize the presence and role of other factors. Religion is always related to and affected by other interests, and it is not surprising that religious conflicts will also carry nonreligious ingredients.

Religious conflicts are also aggravated when a religion is defined by a single ingredient of it. When religion is defined by particular feelings, practices, or beliefs, such as absolute dependence, ultimate concern, the role of the sacred, or the observance of rituals, conflicts between and within religions will likely be aggravated. Conflicts are complicated and more pointed when a defining essence is abstracted from the complexity and dynamics of religion and its context.

In the first part of this book, we looked at the understandings of religion in the work of a diverse selection of representative and influential scholars, and, while appreciative of their scholarly contributions, I also implied that their work had the effect of simplifying religion in order to make it clearer and more manageable. They did this by granting one of the three components of religious systems, namely, what I called the sapiential component, dominance. It is reasonable to suggest that they did this not only because it was clearly dominant in the lives of the religious people they studied but also because they themselves considered religion to be of importance for understanding human cultures when understood primarily in sapiential terms. Emphasis on its sapiential component allows religion more readily to be culturally relevant and positively viewed than would be the case if the prophetic or priestly components were emphasized. It allows religion to be seen not only in its relation to personal and cultural life but also as consistent with and even remedial for it. A similar treatment of religion in terms of the dominance of either of the other two components, prophetic and priestly, would make religion seem more dogmatic and exclusionary.

It follows from this that persons studying religion are faced with the question of whether what I have called a sapiential form of religion can and will do justice to the other two elements of religion and the religious forms that develop when one of the other two and not the sapiential element is dominant. Indeed, it can be expected that those who study religion in academic contexts will themselves act favorably toward forms of religion that are related to the personal, social, and cultural aspects of human life. However, studying religion should also include attention to forms of religion in which one of the other two elements, priestly or prophetic, dominates, and it must also attend to questions raised by the often problematic relations of such forms of religion to cultural and social coherence and stability. Reservations regarding the academic study of religion will arise less when religion is related to human needs, potentials, and well-being than when religion is shaped by the dominance of what cannot be understood or controlled or by occasions and sites taken as loci when or where relations with the transcendent are made possible. When studied, religion should be seen not only in its remedial or beneficial relations to human needs and potentials but also in its potentials to raise questions about and creating difficulties for personal, social, and cultural human interests. As I shall point out later, it is this side of religious studies that should be open to religiously based religious studies where the priestly and prophetic elements of religion will likely carry greater weight.

However, while complexities and difficulties for religious studies are created by the potentially conflicting relations of religion's constitutive components to one another, these components and their relations also serve to avoid or modify religiously based conflicts. The complex nature of religion gives to it internal potentials not only for conflict but also for self-critique because all three components of a religious system can be shown to deserve recognition of their places and their potentials to limit and correct one another. This means that conflict within a religion related to the dominance of one over the other of the components can be modified by giving deserved attention to the subjected components. Dominance is kept from becoming exclusivity because recognition of the other components as legitimate and even necessary is of consequence for preserving the whole. It should also be noticed that critiques of religion may arise more readily concerning excesses of dominance by either of the two other elements, but the sapiential component of religion can also become religiously questionable when a preoccupation with human needs, potentials, and well-being deprives the other two components of their rightful places and roles. While prophetic forms can become culturally disruptive if unmodified by the other components and priestly forms can become occasions for exclusivity and control when unchecked by the other components, so also a sapiential form of a religion, when unchecked by the two other factors, can be reduced to and by reductive and self-serving assumptions concerning what is humanly beneficial. While in Chapter 6, we traced the appearance of priestly and prophetic interests in the work of scholars primarily concerned with the sapiential aspects of religion, those appearances hardly do justice to the potential importance of these other two elements for religious people. Nor, as I suggested, can faculty of the stripe commonly detectable in those hired in the aftermath of the Second World War be counted on to hold up for attention the prophetic and priestly aspects of religion because they were in large part attentive primarily to the sapiential elements in religion, particularly carried by liberal Protestant Christianity.

There are obvious reasons why religion, when present in a conflict, tends to get blamed for it. One is that religious people involved in a conflict with people either of the same religion or of a differing religion often emphasize religious rather than secular motivations and warrants. Religious reasons give more legitimacy to conflict than would more secular reasons. Religion can also confer on other human interests the intensity of feeling and meaning that religious interests carry or sponsor.

Critiques of religion can also, often justifiably, arise because religion can serve as a cover or rationale for the pursuit of nonreligious goals. People critical of religion can understandably be led to think of the religious reasons for the conflict as disguises or excuses for nonreligious causes and aims. Finally, those in religious studies who target religion as divisive and disruptive will likely be, if they are religiously identifiable, sapiential in their religious orientation, that is, concerned primarily with human needs, potentials, and well-being.

Religious studies, in dealing with religious conflict, needs, then, to avoid erring in any of at least three directions. The first is minimizing the virulence with which people who identify with one form of religion can respond to those identified with a differing form of the same or a differing religion. It is hoped that, while not going into more detail as to the reasons for strong religiously based conflicts, enough has been said to indicate why such intensity of involvement can occur. The second error arises from a failure to distinguish between religious and nonreligious factors in a conflict; both kinds of motivations are likely to be present and observable. This will be difficult to do because a people's religion is not easily separable from its nonreligious ingredients. The third error is caused by bringing to the case being studied a preexisting conviction concerning the relations between religious and nonreligious factors in conflicts, thinking one of them to be either secondary or determining.

Finally, while it is possible and in many cases practically wise to emphasize in academic settings the standing and role of religion relative to human needs and potentials, it is important for religious studies to include recognition of the additional components of religion and why their presence is crucial for taking into account the complexities of religions and the dynamics, including negative ones, that these complexities create. This recognition can be aided by the relation of religious studies to the study of religion carried on in religiously identifiable locations.

II

Related to but separable from the internal and external relations of religion to conflict is the complexity of religious studies due to religion's unavoidable interconnections with culture. Implied by the understanding of religion that has been offered here is that religion is always implicated in or affected by its culture while also resisting being taken as wholly accountable to or by it. Differing responses to questions of religion's relations to culture will appear both within a religion and within religious studies. These complexities and potential tensions need to be noted.

Due to its defining marks as favoring sapiential religious interests, religious studies, in its emphasis on human needs and potentials, will take very seriously the interrelations between religion and other aspects of human personal, social, and cultural life. At the same time and in contrast, interests in religion that favor the prophetic and priestly constituents of religion will have less interest in and regard for human factors and even view them as potential contraries and threats to religion. They will view human culture critically because they consider human needs and potentials as subordinate to and in need of correction or replacement by one or the other remaining components. For prophetic systems, the orientation toward what cannot be understood or controlled will intensify the difference between it and human understandings and controls. This will impute to the human condition its being affected by and sponsoring negative factors and forces. For priestly systems, the primary orientation toward the forms of access or relation between what cannot be understood or controlled and the human condition needs to be primary and not human nature or culture mainly understood in and by itself. For both of these systems, religion is basically distinct from human culture and in varying degrees should suspect, challenge, or avoid it rather than determined by it.

For those working with or out of saptiential emphases, prophetic and priestly challenges to human needs and potentials are seen as intrusions into or threats to cultural coherence and advancement and to human freedom, diversity, and relationships. Since sapiential religious systems can be identified as prominent, if not dominant, for the rise and development of modern culture, the progress associated with that culture reinforces the view that religion in its prophetic and priestly forms can hinder those advances. At least since the seventeenth century, the prophetic and priestly elements of religion have played an increasingly limited role in public, including academic, cultural life because they were seen as resisting human progress. A sapiential religious system, with its more general or limited attention to deity, its reduction of priestly authority and religious exclusivity, and its more direct interest in human understanding, advancements, and inter-relations, has increasingly become the privileged form of religion both in modern culture generally and in academic culture particularly.

This cooperative relation between sapiential religious forms and the course of modern development was sharply challenged by historical events that had negative effects on human well-being. While critiques of modernity arose also in nonreligious forms, particularly directed toward the uses and abuses of political and economic power, they had radical consequences for religious studies, for religion itself, and for beliefs concerning the relation of religion and modern culture to one another. Indeed, one of the more important and remarkable developments in the relation of religion to modern culture is the cooperation, often tacit and indirect but real nonetheless, between religious, particularly prophetic and priestly, and nonreligious cultural critiques, especially concerning the dynamics caused by the quest for increased power and control. While not always allied with one another, religious and nonreligious critiques made common cause against the generally optimistic and confident course of modern Western culture. To put it concisely, nonreligious critiques of the culture, epitomized by but not limited to Marxist analyses and correctives, turned on religion in the culture as concealing and warranting forms of exploitation and repression, especially the economic, political, and social repression of some people for the benefit of others and the formation of a culture determined by divisions between the powerful and the exploited and repressed. This theoretical base in the critique of modern culture was symptomatic of and causal for cultural, social, and personal tensions and disruptions that took many forms. These diverse interests were aligned with the already present religious, especially prophetic and priestly, forms of critique of modern culture as well as of human culture itself.

Increasingly in the second quarter of the twentieth century, a mutuality between religious and nonreligious social and cultural critiques came to prominence, particularly in the aftermath of the First World War. The war called radically into question cultural optimism concerning the upward movement of and basic trust in cultural, social, and personal advancement. Voices, both nonreligious and religious, articulated a turn, relative to the culture, from positive to negative assessments. Nonreligious critiques, especially economic and political, found their often tacit agreement with radical shifts in forms of Christian theology of a prophetic and priestly kind, such as those sponsored in Protestantism by the work of Karl Barth and the broader neo-orthodox movement, and in Catholicism, especially in South America, by various forms of Christian Marxism. The differing but often associated critiques of modernity arising from both nonreligious and religious sources continued between the wars supported by broader and diverse developments, including economic depression, the Second World War, other painful and costly military conflicts, and movements that gained visibility in the second half of the twentieth century, such as protests and disruptions aimed at the disparities in social and economic positioning and their relations to race, gender assignments, and the rights and dignities of persons regarded as marginal and objectionable because of their sexual, ethnic, or racial identities.

Such matters, briefly indicated here, altered the course of religious studies and continue to do so. Primarily, they caused or signaled changing understandings of the relations between religion and culture. There are two specific implications of these changes in and for religious studies as presently carried on. The first is an increasingly negative and critical role relative to modern culture taken by religious studies. While we noted in the examples of religious studies offered in the first part of this guide, examples that were used to draw attention to shared and continuing interests in religious studies, the stated and implied critiques of the culture were primarily directed toward its lacks or faults concerning human resources, needs, and worldviews. While constituting a critique of modernity, these appraisals can be seen as comparatively mild in effect and remedial in intention relative to the more radical and culturally challenging religious critiques and their relations to nonreligious critiques in the course of religious studies during the closing decades of the previous and the opening decades of the present century. It is not too much to say that religious studies as presently engaged is culturally directed more noticeably toward critical than toward positive or remedial ends. But the heavily critical and negative direction and spirit of religious and cultural studies turns attention away from challenges and opportunities that have been and, it can be argued, should be retained as part of the agenda, namely, to find in the culture those aspects of it deserving positively to be assessed and pursued. The present situation creates a challenge to locate where and when critiques of religion become so acidic for the culture as to erode or neglect its roles for clarifying human values and ameliorating cultural tensions and ills. Expectations of a more positive approach to the existence and role of the shared culture, both academic and general, will not be encouraged by the continuing directions of both determined, as seems increasingly the case, by materialism in its various forms. One of the challenges to religious studies is to supplement or even counter this direction by opening accesses to positive alternatives for both religion and late modernity, for their relations, supportive as well as corrective, to one another.

An important change for religious studies attributable to the altered assessment of modernity is that the separation and even contrary relations between religious studies with its dominantly sapiential form and confessional or institutionally based religious studies with their more dominantly prophetic and priestly forms have been altered. The accusation on the part of more traditional or confessional religious stances that religious studies relied in the past on an uncritical optimism and sentimental humanism can be altered now by the contrary observation that cultural critique in religious studies may be falling under the spell of academic materialism in its various forms. Religious studies can be enriched by joining with more prophetic and priestly forms of religious interests in developing an understanding of and approach to human needs and potentials that deliver religious studies from the threat of being limited to and determined by the materialism that is increasingly pervasive in current, especially critical, academic culture.

This second source of complexity for religious studies, namely, determining and clarifying the relation of religion to culture and religious studies to cultural studies, will cause uncertainty and tensions, and even conflict. Not all will agree on religion's complicity in aggravating personal, social, and cultural problems and ills, and not all will agree on the trustworthiness and adequacy of nonreligious options for addressing cultural needs and potentials. Perhaps most importantly, not all will agree on the need for an increased rapprochement between religious studies and more explicitly formed prophetic or priestly oriented religious interests. But the pressures for religious and cultural changes and their relations to one another have been and are increasingly occurring, and they require discernment vital for the viability and stability of religious studies in current academic culture.

III

A third cause of complexity and dissonance in and for religion and the study of it arises from the fact that religions are both particular and, at the same time, similar and comparable to one another. The tendency may easily arise to favor one of these options at the expense of the others, to treat religions as distinct or to treat them as basically similar or even the same. This difference can give rise to contrary methods in the study of religion.

One method tends to treat religions as unlike in form but alike in essence. It is an approach that tries to cut through the complexities and differences of people's religious beliefs and practices in order to expose a shared core, an essence by which religions can basically be identified. At times, this core is granted a causal role, making the development or diversification of a religion secondary. The definition of religion central to this guide to some degree shares this kind of approach because of the argument that identifying the constitutive components of religion is not confined or determined by one religion but, in varying degrees, is relevant to all.

Holding together the similarities between religions and their particularities is aggravated by a further question, namely, whether the nature or cause of religion is to be found in religion itself or is to be found in something in addition to or other than religion. This is a persistent question because religion, while it needs to be distinguishable from other aspects of human lives and cultures, is also always affected by or intertwined with them, including psychological, social, political, and aesthetic factors. These attachments not only complicate religious studies but also enrich them. However, they give rise to the question of which determines which. To use a simple analogy, we can ask which, religion or culture, is, let us say, the magnet and which the metal filings. Is it religion that attracts and attaches itself to other aspects of life and gives them their roles and shape, or are these other aspects the magnet that attracts and shapes religion? Locating or accounting for religion is, therefore, a complicated and even contentious matter, but it also enriches religious studies. Again, it is a complexity that, while involving other matters, arises from the nature and roles of religion itself. It will not do to reduce complexities by treating religion not as something more or other than its roles and effects on various aspects of lives and cultures because religion would then simply be a name given to various human interests and activities. One is left with the complexities raised by the fact that religion is implicated in or embodied by a variety of particular human and cultural factors while also being something that is detectable and separable from them, something that primarily relates its various factors to one another. People have all kinds of beliefs and practices that are important to them, but not all, even if intensely held or rigorously practiced, are religious. Difficulties arise inevitably from the need to treat religion both as variously and particularly embedded in human lives and cultures and also as separable from them and related to what can be taken as religious in the lives of differing peoples and in human life generally considered. It also seems inevitable that some scholars in religious studies will pay primary attention to the standing and roles of religion as it is embedded or manifested in particular forms of human interest and culture while others, starting at the alternative end, will approach religion primarily as something separable from the varieties of human interests and cultures that attach themselves to it. These two approaches can be combined, but they also represent distinguishable methods, the one primarily theoretical, even when it is also descriptive or historical, and the other primarily descriptive or historical, even when it carries analytic or theoretical ingredients.

Another property of religion that creates complexities and tensions in and for the study of it is that people adhere to their religion with an emphasis on one of three aspects of it: religious actions or practices, beliefs or assumptions, or feelings or emotions. Any of these three can be dominant for a religion, for individuals and groups identifying with the same religion, and for the study of religion. It should be kept in mind, however, that when one of these three foci of religious life is taken as dominant, this may be due to the interests of the investigator in that particular focus. The examples of religious studies at which we looked emphasize one more than another of these three possibilities, and they may well do so not because the one selected is actually the one emphasized by the religion but because the scholar by training or interest is drawn to it. Actions are more observable than beliefs and feelings, but beliefs can also be taken as dominant for religious people. Although they are less accessible to study, especially when a religion lacks central texts, they are always present. In traditional societies, beliefs tend to be embedded and not deliberately formulated, abstracted, and related to one another. Western students of religion, familiar as they may be with Protestant Christianity, likely will expect to encounter religious beliefs because articulating beliefs is an important agenda of Christianity generally and of Protestantism particularly. Feelings and emotions, which constitute the third aspect of religious life, are even more elusive and various, and attention to them in the study of religion is largely inferential and dependent on the testimony of the people studied. In addition, there is always some continuity or similarity between religious and other human feelings and emotions. It is noteworthy that religious studies as we know it, which arose in the context of Romanticism and its strong emphasis on personal emotions and feelings, often focus on such matters in accounts of the standing and role of religion in human lives. A focus on feelings also allows for particularity and similarity to be combined. Mystical experiences, for example, can be studied in both particular and comparative or general terms. As already mentioned, an important redirection in Protestant religious thought was introduced by Friedrich Schleiermacher in the period of high Romanticism when he made religious feeling, primarily the feeling of absolute dependence, the ground of religion from which beliefs, practices, and institutions arise. The complexities of a religion caused by these three forms of expression, beliefs, practices, and feelings, should not be lessened by excluding one or another of them, but it is likely that a religious person or group and a scholar in religious studies will be more attentive to one of the three than to the other two.

It should be mentioned that there has been a shift in religious studies away from attention to religious beliefs to religious practices and feelings. While this shift in attention was warranted and needed, a case can be made that it now places interests in the study of religious beliefs in too much of a secondary position. Without taking away the importance of attention to religious practices, artifacts, sites, and feelings, it should be clear that beliefs also are or can be as important and determining for religious people. I mention this not only as an assessment of a shift of attention that may well have been too extreme or radical but also as a shift that needs correction if religion in religious studies is to retain its integrity. Some of the more recent emphases on religious practices, sites, and artifacts, in other words on what is often called "material religion," need to protect themselves from the extreme of understanding religion causally and essentially in materialist terms. A major agenda item for the future of religious studies should be reassessing the standing and role of beliefs and their articulation in and for religious people, especially beliefs in what in a very general way I referred to as "what cannot be understood or controlled," that is, the transcendent, the spiritual, and the mysterious, and their standing and roles relative to human needs and potentials.

IV

I have selected three general kinds of complexities and excesses in and for religious studies today that should be kept in mind as obvious and extending into the future. This choice is not insistent; there may be other matters that deserve equal or more attention and concern. But these three are worth noting.

One is the question of the causal relations of religion to conflict both within particular religions and between them and the relation of religious to nonreligious factors in conflicts. A second is the shift in assessments from both religious and nonreligious perspectives of modern culture and its relation to human needs and potentials. To what extent can and should religious studies be aligned with the cultural critique of modernity that arises from nonreligious and identifiable materialist methods and assumptions? A third complexity arises from the question of how religion should be approached. Is a religion to be studied in its particularity, or should it be approached as similar to and even the same as other religions. It is hoped that this selection of complexities, while not exhaustive, indicates that religious studies, while needing an identity more unifying and firm than is presently the case, will also not, and need not, be delivered from the differences and tensions created by the complexities of religion and the problems to which they may lead.

Chapter 8

STUDYING RELIGION WHILE BEING RELIGIOUS

It follows from what has been said that one's own religion, while also particular, resembles other religions in many ways. It is like them as being constituted actually or potentially by the three components of a religious system. It is also like them because religions will find expression in practices, beliefs, and/or feelings. And it is like others because some kinds of relations, positive and negative, will be assumed to exist between a religion and its cultural context. For these and other reasons at which we have looked, it becomes clear that, if a person studying religion is religious, the question of the relation between who the person is and what is being studied arises. This question arises in various forms and is answered in a variety of ways. Addressing even some forms of the question and the answers to it that could be given would be too extensive a task. Indeed, it is a matter which, while having some general status, is and should remain largely personal, although it should also be acknowledged and examined.

I

Among the world's major religions, Christianity, while not alone in this regard, is noticeable as having a tradition marked by frequent and often intense differences and even conflicts both between Christians and between them and others. This by itself would warrant selecting Christianity as the occasion for considering some aspects of this matter. But it is also the major religion in Western history and culture, and that history and cultural context are densely marked by differences and conflicts. It seems justifiable, then, to take it as a way of addressing the wider question of the relations between the religion one studies and one's own religion.

As mentioned earlier, the question of the relation between Christians and between them and people of other religions is central already from the start because Christianity arose in the context of close relations to other religions, particularly Judaism. Adherents of early Christianity were not in agreement with one another concerning the relations of their own religion to the Jewish context in which it arose. This question was intensified and made more urgent by the fact that early Christians were also included in a political, cultural, and economic empire that had its own religion or religions. The principal response of early Christians concerning this question was to affirm Christianity less as continuous with the religions around them than as contrary to them. Aggravating the situation was the fact that Christians exhibited from the outset a more pronounced interest in converting others than did either Jews or adherents of Greek and Roman religions. Interest in converting others revealed a conviction within Christian beliefs and practices not only of difference from other religions but also of superior status relative to them.

Christianity, when set in a contrary relation to Judaism, was so distinct that the God of Judaism and the God of Christianity were taken by some to be not the same. Others moved more in the direction of continuity, seeing being Christian as a way of continuing to be Jewish. A major question arising from the conversion of Jewish neighbors to Christianity was whether or not they should first become Jews, specifically whether it was necessary for them to undergo circumcision on their way to becoming Christian. On the question of Greek and Roman religions, the response was more implicit, allowing Christians to be variously related to people in the cultural context, such as eating food that had been included in religious rituals. In other words, Christianity did not take a clear and shared stand on the question of its continuity or discontinuity with other religions but displayed a number of responses between the clear alternatives of continuity and discontinuity.

When in the fourth century Christianity became the state religion, it took on an official and political standing that gave the need to settle this question a secondary status. While recurring differences and conflicts within Christianity arose, some of which were threats to unity, institutional unity became dominant until the separation between the Eastern or Orthodox churches and Western Christianity in the eleventh century. Western Christianity remained relatively unified institutionally until the so-called Reformation, which resulted in a variety of Christian institutions that were to some degree also distinguishable politically and ethnically. This radical change from a strongly dominant form of Christianity to many differing institutions turned the question of discontinuity and continuity more fully toward the relation of one's own religious identity to differing kinds of Christians, a question that was intensified by political and cultural differences. Differences between kinds of Christians encouraged the formation of religious identity as contrary and even oppositional. Differences between Christians either made the question of the relation of Christianity to other religions less immediate and urgent or made the question easier to answer, namely, that if other kinds of Christians were different, wrong, and needing to be resisted or changed, this was certainly the case with non-Christians. The spread of Western interests into distant areas and cultures in early modernity was not only accompanied by an assumption of the superiority of Christianity relative to other religions but was also a legitimization of the subjugation of other societies and their cultures to Western interests.

As proposed earlier in this guide, attitudes toward the cultures of other peoples, including their religions, changed, most noticeably in the eighteenth and early nineteenth centuries, a change that contributed to the rise of religious studies as we know it today. As we have seen, religious studies arose in the context of more positive academic interests in people distant both in time and in location from Western modernity. This change was also supported by the understandings of religion implied by religious studies, understandings that I have labeled sapiential. In sapiential religious formations, Christianity, especially when influenced by biblical wisdom literature, took a more positive and even appreciative attitude toward other cultures and their religions, which could be seen as part of the more general interest taken by biblical wisdom literature in human needs, potentials, and well-being.

Cultural change also occurred regarding this question. Diversity in populations, cultural and economic relations between differing societies and cultures, and newer forms of communication and transportation have given support to an increasingly important role in Western culture of a more neutral and even more positive understanding of religious differences, although, one should add, this change in attitude is also due to declining cultural conviction regarding the relevance of religion to human well-being and advancement, a process housed under the general term "secularization."

A conclusion to be drawn from all of this is that there is little sign of an explicit and shared position among Christians as to the relation of their own religion and form of it to other forms of Christianity as well as other religions. Today, the answers Christians give to the question of the relation of their own religion to other religions vary greatly. At one end of the spectrum are people who apply the designation "religion" to all but Christianity, implying that Christianity is not one of many religions but is a rendering of and response to what is actually and truly the case. At the other end of the spectrum are those for whom Christianity is a religion that provides what other religions in their differing ways also provide to their adherents. To call one of these two responses or any answer located between them "the Christian answer" serves less as an answer than as an indicator of the position of the person offering the response.

Given this situation, it is incumbent on religious persons teaching religion, and perhaps especially on Christians, to recognize what is being assumed regarding how relations to other religions and studying them affect and are affected by the student's own religious identity. If a student of religion has no religious identity, this should also be recognized because a nonreligious stance, even when presented as a form of neutrality, is an active alternative to religious stances. A nonreligious alternative is not neutral but rests on a decision relative to religion that should be acknowledged.

Given these conditions, it seems appropriate to expose my own response to the question of engaging in religious studies while also being religious, in this case, a Christian. As a preface to my account, I can say that I try to place myself in a location that avoids the contrary extremes of the spectrum. In response to the one extreme, it is obvious to me that Christianity is, for reasons such as those I have given, a religion that in fundamental ways is like others, however much it also differs from them. Also, Christianity, like other religions, takes form in particular human cultures, and forms of Christianity differ not only for the structural and dynamic reasons I have given but also because of cultural and personal differences. On the contrary extreme, I find a position that treats Christianity as one of many doors to the same room or one of many paths to the same mountaintop uncertain because there is no position above all religions that makes such a view of them and their common role or goal reasonable. While religions are, especially structurally, similar to one another, they are not versions of the same thing. This makes possible the conclusion that Christianity, because it is also a religion, can be related to and compared with other religions while also being unlike them.

It should also be said that the question of the relation of being a Christian to people who religiously differ can make a Christian studying religion aware of how important for them the religions of other people are. This is, I think, a great advantage for studying religion. A nonreligious student of religion will find it more difficult to recognize what being religious means for those being studied than will a religious student of religion. For a nonreligious student of religion, what is being studied will have to be taken as something less or other than those being studied take it to be. A case can be made that one's own religion can increase the chances for an understanding of and appreciation for the religion of someone else that is as strong as the case made that the religious identity of the person studying religion counters or dilutes an understanding and appreciation of the religions of others.

However, it is also the case that religious identity can produce indifference and even hostility toward those of differing religious identities. There are conditions that help to produce this stance. One is that it is more likely to appear in those whose religious identities are more prophetic or priestly than sapiential. Another is that a positive attitude toward those of differing religions need not be taken as a sign suggesting a lack of conviction or loyalty. In my opinion, a third condition is the most influential cause of religious intolerance toward adherents of other religions. It is the practice of securing identity by means of opposition. This means of identification, while not limited to Western modernity, is certainly characteristic of it. It is not too much to say that in this culture identity is primarily not only personal but also oppositional. It is easier to clarify identity by asserting what one is not than by saying what one is. This means that opposition toward people of a differing religion is more likely to be culturally than it is to be religiously caused. At least one should be aware of this condition and willing to recognize its consequences.

Finally, it should be pointed out that a religious person studying religion can make a common cause with religiously differing people because in the present culture they share a common contrary, namely, culturally assumed or deliberately formed and applied materialism. Religious people can share the conviction or are susceptible to the proposal that being human and having a workable worldview require more than what is provided by an understanding that has as its basis the final reality and causal sufficiency of matter and energy. While we live in a culture, both general and academic, that, for reasons I listed earlier, makes it easy to think that what is real is material and that what is not material is conjectural, lacking a defensible base and adequate account, the student of religion can share with the religious people being studied and with others who study religion that something more or other than material is necessary. Materialism as an adequate account of ourselves and the human world is a difficult case to make even while it appears, increasingly so, to be a cultural assumption in late modernity that serves to account for what is and occurs without needing to be defended.

In response to the question of the relation of being religious to studying religion, I shall, rather than attempt an answer to this question that could be adopted by others, describe a way by which my exposure to religious studies affected my own religious identity. I use this personal example also because I think that answers to the questions we are here addressing are related to and affected by personal experience. In my case, three moments stand out.

II

I was raised in a conservative religious culture, one shaped by my father's position as pastor in a Dutch Reformed Church. His direct influence on me was abruptly altered by his death when I, the youngest of four children, was eight years old, but the stamp or mold was clear and firm. I pursued my education with the expectation that I would carry on my father's work in Christian ministry also because my two older brothers had a negative interest in doing so themselves.

My undergraduate education in a college with a clear Reformed or Calvinist identity was for the most part strong, especially in the ways in which Christianity was taken not as a basis for separation from intellectual and cultural inquiry and enrichment but as integral to them. But when I entered the denominational seminary, which when I entered it was in a low state due to faculty retirements and firings, I found it to be oriented primarily toward the inculcation of Reformed theology in isolation from and opposition to and not in relation to other forms of Christianity and, even less, to other religions. My experience there led me to the conclusion that I should not enter the ministry in the denomination because it was largely determined, counter to its tradition, by centripetal dynamics that made more of separation and enclosure than of openness and engagement.

Two things prevented me from leaving behind the religious content of my background when I entered the graduate program in religion at the University of Chicago. First, I encountered there an orthodoxy as firm as it was different from what I had known before, namely, process theology, something that as a philosophy would have engaged me but as a theology did not. The two theological systems could hardly differ more from one another, but both were rationally based and firmly institutionalized. Second, early on I read, among other influential texts, Rudolf Otto's *The Idea of the Holy*.

Readers acquainted with the scholars used in the first part of this guide as examples in a tradition of interests in religious studies may have noticed that I did not include Otto. I did not partly because he is somewhat different from the others in the extent to which he included Christianity in his theory of what is central to and causative of religion generally. In addition, he emphasized similarities across religions based on a kind of experience that is unique, stands apart from, and is immediately taken as contrary to what is humanly constructed or controlled. In other words, his theory lies more in a direction toward a prophetic understanding of religion than toward a more clearly sapiential orientation of the scholars I used as examples.

Otto was educated in a Christian, particularly orthodox Lutheran, context, and he moved from that base first into philosophy and then into the study of South Asian religions. His philosophical focus was Kantian, and he attended in his study of religion primarily to Hinduism. His book on the "Holy," which was published in English in the 1920s and widely read, contained examples not only from the texts and practices of other religions but also from Christian sources, especially biblical texts. This inclusion implies his critique of Christianity, especially in its orthodox Protestant forms, namely, that it had been given over too heavily to rational, institutional, and ethical formations. The principal effect on me of this widely influential book was to emphasize the non- or extra-rational in religion, including Christianity.

Otto's treatment of the nonrational in religion was given philosophical support by the role of the *a priori*, the role for human understanding and experience of what in the mind is a precondition for perceiving and knowing but cannot itself be known or perceived. It is a capacity that awaits awakening by something that comes to it from without. An experience or perception of something is a compound, then, formed by the coming together of an innate capacity and an external stimulus. This emphasis in Otto is augmented by his philosophical attention to intuition, the ability, that is, to recognize the validity or reality of something not because it is empirically or rationally demonstrable but because the validity or reality of other matters depends upon it. Other aspects of Otto's culture contributed to the influence of his work, particularly Kant's theories of the sublime. What also grabbed my interest was that Otto makes a specific connection between his own theory of religion and Romanticism, particularly by means of his declared dependence on the work of Friedrich Schleiermacher, who a century earlier gave to feeling, particularly the feeling of dependence, centrality in his radical reformulation of Christianity. Otto's response to Schleiermacher's formulation was to say that, while sound, it was inadequate because Schleiermacher's proposal placed too much weight on an internal experience. It was important for Otto to establish that religious experience, like the experience of the sublime, arises from or finds a place in not only something within the person but also from something that comes from without and to which religious feeling is a response. He called the experience that is basic to religion the experience of the Holy.

The experience of the Holy has, for Otto, two aspects or components. While he seems to have wanted to give equal status to both sides, the one, which is rational and suggests attributes of deity such as goodness, is less emphasized than the other, which is nonrational and that he called the *numinous*. The nonrational also has two aspects, the *tremendum*, which is dreadful and forbidding, and the *fascinans*, which is captivating and intriguing. He makes the nonrational aspect of the experience of the Holy, the *numinous*, dominant for three reasons. First, the rational seems to be a second-level response to the Holy, a conscious formulation of theological and moral principles. Second, the nonrational seems to hold a critical position relative to the rational, since it seems that a religion can become too rational more readily than too nonrational, a point that seems to implicate Protestant orthodoxy. Finally, the experience of the *numinous* can be recognized in many, if not all, religions, while the rational side of religion creates differences both between and within religions that cannot be readily reconciled. Indeed, he takes awareness and experience of the *numinous* to be a characteristic that is human-making and *sui generis*. While it relates to other experiences, like fear or desire, it cannot be explained in their terms. Critics of Otto, of which there are many in the field of religious studies, complain particularly about this moment in his work since it places religious experience not only in a category of its own but also beyond description. But it should be remembered that Otto's positing of the *sui generic* character of the experience of the *numinous* is based on his understanding of the role of the *a priori* in epistemology, the importance of intuited axioms, the continuing cultural interest in the sublime, and the common difficulty that people have in finding language adequate for describing experiences that are unusual, profound, or life-changing for them.

I was impressed, even altered, by reading *The Idea of the Holy* not only because Otto included biblical examples but also because it made me aware of why the Christianity with which I had grown up had come to look sterile to me. It also clarified, at least partially, why the form of Christianity that dominated my upbringing could be taken by many of its adherents as not only certain but also as sharply different both from other forms of Christianity and from other religions. While my Calvinist background had instilled a sense of the august standing of deity, this awareness was translated by Otto from a theological idea into a new kind of awareness.

An additional theological turn should also be mentioned, namely, my encounters with neo-orthodox Christian theology or Barthianism that were brought to a head by the extended visit to the university by Karl Barth. This form of Christian theology represents, among much else, a recoil from modernity and from human culture in general because of its having been discredited primarily by the impact of the First World War. It focused attention on Christianity's own integrity and sufficiency removed from culture and located in revelation. The transcendence of Christianity relative to human culture was implied, and this stress on the independence of Christianity from human culture also carried with it a separation from other things human. This assertive and clear form of Christian theology was appealing to me for several reasons: it had a pervasive and quickening effect on theological interests in this country; it carried a good bit of what Otto called the *numinous*; it fit well with the critique of Western modernity that I took not only from my Calvinist background but also from the modern artists and cultural critics I had been studying; and it clarified my desire for an alternative to the pervasive influence at Chicago of philosophically grounded process theologies. But gradually I distanced myself from Barthianism, a distancing that was completed by my exposure to what could be called radical orthodoxy when it appeared in particularly aggressive forms. It was not only the acerbic and isolationist qualities of this form of Christianity but also its self-definition as a contrary not only to modern culture generally but also to forms of Christianity affected by modern culture for which I had developed a more appreciative attitude. I had formed an understanding of and regard for forms of Christianity that I came to identify as sapiential, forms that I concluded were not simply distortions or reductions of orthodox or traditional Christianity but having their own integrity, textual sources, and tradition.

While the appeal of Barthianism faded for me, Otto's impact continued, not because I was wholly convinced by his positioning of the experience of the Holy as the causative basis of religions but because he made me aware of how my relation to other religions and to religious studies could be positive and even corrective. Otto made me aware, then, not only that there were important similarities between Christianity and other religions but also that such similarities could allow one to become aware and more appreciative of counterparts in one's own religion. While not a point of Otto's that all would share but that is shared by many of the scholars that were earlier discussed, I was encouraged by him in taking religion not as something odd or exceptional in human life and cultures but as, if not a human-making characteristic, something deeply and pervasively embedded. I also realized that the formative role of religion in my own identity could aid me in understanding the role of other religions in the lives of their adherents. Being religious became, then, not a hindrance to but an asset for studying it.

III

Another way by which my religious identity was positively affected by religious studies was the exposure it provided to the continuing importance of religion in and for modernity. I earlier had thought of deistic, humanistic, or Romantic forms of religion generally and of Christianity particularly to be watered down, partial, or humanly determined. This attitude was enforced by the influence of Ludwig Feuerbach (1804–1872) for whom theological ideas, especially of God, are projections of human self-images. However, I came to see that the disparagement of so-called liberal Christianity depended on a caricature of it and on an inadequate understanding not only of religion but also of Christianity. Liberal, culturally concerned, and humanistic forms of Christianity were not of necessity to be taken as compromised versions of something else but forms that, although also at times diluted and even slipping into something less or other than Christianity or even religion, had their own textual sources, complexity, and integrity.

I recognized that I had viewed so-called liberal Christianity from a standpoint determined by a prophetic form of it. As I have tried to point out, it is inevitable that one form of any religion, including Christianity, will tend to sponsor negative views of the other two forms. I carried a disparaging attitude toward "modernist" or "liberal" Christianity because I inherited a religious form dominated by its prophetic factor. What I came to realize is that Christianity in its more culturally engaged and humanly directed forms should be understood as having its own integrity, reputable history, and a biblical basis. Those who espouse it emphasize the role of religion in addressing human needs, potentials, and well-being and providing people with an understanding of their world, their positions in it, and their relations within and to it. Christian critics of sapiential forms of the tradition likely view it from a position that is priestly or prophetic and see its attention to human needs and potentials as a reductive subjection of Christianity to humanist interests and constructions.

It is not only prophetic and priestly adherents of Christianity who are critical of sapiential forms. I found that members of academic culture also tended to dismiss sapiential forms of religion as halfway stops toward that to which, it is thought, they inevitably lead, namely, to humanism and, perhaps, materialism. I recall a conversation I had with a member of the political science department about the role of religion in the work of John Locke. When I pointed out the interest that Locke took in Christianity, which included his commentaries on the Pauline epistles, he dismissed that part of Locke as transitional or vestigial and separable from and irrelevant to the basically secular direction and outcome of his philosophical and political thought. One detects this kind of impatience in anti-religious critics of sapiential religion because this form of religion does not provide the kind of clear basis they need to make their critiques, such as religion's characteristic forms of repressive and obstructive authority, forceful. Radical critiques of religion can be more accurately aimed at forms that are more specific and dogmatic than sapiential forms tend to be. Sapiential religion is subject to dismissal from both religious and nonreligious sides because it seems not to be religious enough.

I argued, in response, that sapiential religious systems in Christian and other traditions are not only valid religious forms but also prominent participants in the formation of Western modernity. I also pointed out that the sources and warrants of this form were provided primarily by biblical wisdom literature. Focusing on Christianity, I tried to show, as I indicated in the opening chapter of this book, that this religious form, while always part of the tradition, came to prominence in the late sixteenth and early seventeenth centuries and eventually became culturally dominant.

No one of the three forms of religion is necessarily less religious than the other two. All three forms are vulnerable to excesses and distortions. Prophetic forms, oriented as they are to the primacy and power of what cannot be understood or controlled, can, as I indicated earlier, allow adherents in their fervor to apply to themselves some of the primacy and authority characteristic of that by which they believe themselves to be commissioned. They, in the name of that for which they act or speak, call down judgment on human constructions as monuments to arrogance. Priestly forms of Christianity become excessive when they are so attentive to the locations and means by which beneficial access to what cannot be understood or controlled is made available to people that they become more attentive to the means of access than to that to which access is granted. Turning in the other direction, they may well extend the authority or power derived from the means of access to the entire realm of human initiatives and interests, including political. Such excesses—and others could be cited—are difficult to avoid, and they make religion an easy target for those who object to religion because it leads to fanaticism and intolerance or because its authority creates obstacles to cultural advancements.

No less are sapiential forms of religion subject to excess and distortion. This comes about primarily by a preoccupation with human needs and potentials, particularly with accounts of the world and one's relations to and within it, a preoccupation that can lack adequate attention to what cannot be understood or controlled or to the benefits that are made available to people by forms believed to provide access to the transcendent. Sapiential forms of religion, because they are, more than the other two forms, oriented to and by the culture in which they exist, can lose their prophetic and priestly components altogether. When that occurs, they lose their critical distance relative to the cultures in which they are implicated and become determined by them.

When I came to appreciate what I am calling a sapiential form as both a constitutive part of Christianity and a major factor within modern culture, I began to recognize its power and appeal and to see my own religious identity quickened by it. I began to see a sapiential form of Christianity as itself a viable option and not an attenuated form of Christianity or the subjection of religion to the authority of human interests, especially the rational, technological, and scientific advances of modernity.

A related moment of quickening by religious studies in my relation to Christianity was exposure to the effects on human lives of the brute power that marks so much of nineteenth and twentieth century Western history and comes to a head in political forms and in the World Wars and other conflicts. Indeed, I came to accept the exposure of the human desire for power at the expense of others as integral to modernity. Given the negative theological anthropology of my Calvinist background, I was predisposed to draw this conclusion, but I also was able to relate to the exposure of human baseness and seediness made available in and through the work of modern literary artists and cultural historians and critics.

I was also made appreciative of the postwar rise to prominence of interest in religion generally, in Asian religions, and, more particularly, in Buddhism.

This revival had behind it a history of preparation that can be traced to the Romantic enchantment with the East and, during the Victorian period, the popularization of Eastern religion, as, for example, in the rise of such movements as Theosophy, in the spread of other forms of religious spiritualism toward the end of the nineteenth century, and in expanding American interest in mysticism and spiritual practices associated with but not limited to New England. Particular and notable manifestations of the turn to the East included the work of American writers and seekers after truth, who epitomized a general cultural turn in America toward the East. Indeed, like so many people at the time, I read with interest the work of D. T. Suzuki and was intrigued by the positive views of Buddhism in European as well as American writers such as Hesse and Kerouac, and the interest of influential Christians like Thomas Merton in Buddhism. I saw in modernity the signs of correction and renewal drawn from recognizable religious sources. My conclusion, that a sapiential form of religion was potentially as resilient and culturally critical as prophetic and priestly forms, kept me from allowing modern culture to discredit sapiential Christianity.

The critical conclusion I drew from the cultural rise of interest in religion and the study of it and in the roles of prophetic and priestly forms of Christianity was that materialism, both theoretical and cultural, formed a major contributor to the negative characteristics of modernity. I began to see cultural reaffirmations of the spiritual and ideal not as eccentric or desperate but as serious attempts to counter the reductive and ultimately destructive consequences of materialism for human culture and for the relations of modern people within and to their worlds. I came to see literary culture, religious studies, and other religious traditions, despite their obvious differences from my own Christian identity, unified by the conviction that we cannot, with impunity, give ourselves over for redefinition to the interests of those who advance a culture exclusively or dominantly construed materialistically.

IV

Returning to the first half of this guide, I can now add that I treated the rise of religious studies in the ways that I did for two reasons. One is that I want to suggest that the three kinds of interests or topics revealed in the work of selected theorists and researchers reveal ways by which religion, including Christianity, especially in its sapiential forms, can be relevant to modern, including academic, culture. The other is to make us more aware of the lacks and faults of modernity that these texts bring to light by drawing attention to the religious beliefs and practices of people that these texts make available. This implies that people who self-identify as religious can benefit from and enrich their identities by treating their own religion as relevant to modernity in ways made available by religious studies. They can recognize ways in which other religions, as we have seen them presented by the various studies at which we looked, call attention to human needs and potentials that are relevant to and remedial also for modern culture. By responding to modernity's lacks and faults and suggesting the correcting or restoring potentials that the religious beliefs and practices of other cultures offer, they also suggest the value of viewing one's own culture as related in complex ways to religion.

The first set of interests in the rise and directions of religious studies is readiness to identify and support what would serve to make the human world less painful and more beneficial but is neglected or repressed by the cultural will for power, advancement, and self-interest. One factor that can be monitored is the prominent, if not defining, preoccupation of modernity with progress, increase, and acquisition and the resulting neglect and even repression of human potentials and needs that are underappreciated and ameliorating for a culture. A culture should be evaluated not only by what is achieved and acquired but also by what is neglected, marginalized, or repressed. Preoccupation with advance tends to leave valuable matters behind or to brush them aside in its wake. Without rehearsing what has already been said about theorists and researchers who reveal awareness of the prophetic component of religion, their studies of religious people remind us that the forward direction of a culture can easily neglect that from which it has come and to which it is indebted, that a preoccupation with the acquisition and increase of power neglects and disregards those who are made to look unimportant and irrelevant. This disregard can and does arise not only in relation to human needs and potentials but also to the larger natural environment and context of our lives. Much that is neglected or undervalued by modernity and that has been and can be brought to attention by religious studies could be cited. Let it suffice to say that there are always important matters, needs, and potentials that a culture, in its preoccupation with progress and power, tends to undervalue and even repress.

In addition to such prophetic matters, there are the priestly matters to which religious studies call attention, namely, intangibles that people, both individually and communally, need and to which religion can and does grant access. Religious people can find bases for responding positively to the need for having meaningful purpose and direction in their lives, a sense of unity with and affirmation of others, and a feeling of being not isolated from the world but of being a part of it. Such "priestly" matters, access to intangibles that in any case are needed, should be brought to awareness and deployed in and by religious studies.

Finally, religion in its sapiential forms can contribute substantially to the provision of more adequate worldviews, a sense of the coherence and complexity of our world, and the role of directives as to what our relations to and within it could and should be. Rather than bringing the world into oneself or under one's own jurisdiction, religion and studying religion can allow us to become an integral part of a world viewed as something more comprehensive and meaningful than is a view based mainly on personal or group identities and interests. Religion offers not only more adequate worldviews but also worldviews that, at least potentially, are less reductive and more edifying, less oriented toward and by power, and more toward and by values and wisdom. Crucial for understanding what is required by an adequate worldview is the recognition that it is based not only on what is materially or rationally grounded but also on what is believed. Religious beliefs are kinds of beliefs, and all beliefs, religious and nonreligious, that form the worldviews of persons, groups, and cultures should be a matter of diagnostic and prescriptive importance for religious studies.

These three interests in, aspects of, and directives for religious studies can enrich, enliven, and complicate the religious lives of those engaged in and by it. Affirming them requires viewing one's own religion first of all as open to religious studies and to the contributions of religious people who are different. This does not mean that for students of religion their own religion must become just another religion. But if it is taken to be more than that, it must also be seen as related to other religions and to human culture.

Finally, a matter of continuing awareness in religious studies should be the character and direction of modern Western culture. The depiction of the rise of religious studies in this guide draws attention to a prominent characteristic of modernity as it begins to reveal itself during the close of the eighteenth and the opening decades of the nineteenth century and is fully exposed today. It is a culture increasingly determined not only by human understanding and control but by the reduction of the human world to what helps to make it understandable and controllable, namely, materiality, that is, matter and energy or power. While more explicit in some than in others among the theorists and researchers we surveyed, they, in differing ways and to varying degrees, display religion as a challenge, alternative, or supplement to a culture that is determined by materialism, determined, that is, by assumptions that posit power and control as offering the primary terms by which to understand our world, our relations to and within it, and ourselves.

CONCLUSION

It is hoped that this guide to the study of religion has made clear that there are two major paths that can be followed in what has generally come to be called religious studies: a path that is religiously based and a path that is nonreligious or secular. I have tried to account for the presence of the two paths and to call for a response to their separation. Now, in conclusion, I shall repeat my opinion that the choice should be made for a third, less traveled, path between the two that makes possible an easing of the separation between them by means of a shared ground. I propose this path because I think that the present separation makes the academic study of religion or religious studies vulnerable to being absorbed by one or the other of these two sides. I have tried to make clear, both by tracing the field historically and by addressing some issues in it theoretically, a path for sharing concerns that both sides, actually or potentially, contain, namely, a focus on and concern for human needs, potentials, and well-being. In addition, I think that this proposal will give the study of religion a clearer and more secure academic role than is presently the case. A department of religious studies has three options: to conform to the nonreligious and increasingly materialist methods and assumptions of academic culture; to assume or retain a religious identity, either single or plural; or to establish its own role and identity between these alternatives.

In this conclusion, I shall add some comments on each of these three options. First, I shall comment on methodological and theoretical materialism and why it does not provide adequate terms for a department dedicated to the study of religion. Second, I shall comment briefly on the religiously based option. Finally, I shall summarize the goal of this book, namely, to clarify a way by which the identity of a department of religious studies can distinguish itself from the alternatives on both sides and yet retain positive relations with them.

I

Throughout this guide, I have used the term "materialism" to describe the nonreligious or secular option. I do this because I think that this is finally to what a nonreligious option leads. I also do so because materialism is pervasive in both academic and general culture. One could say that it has been naturalized, that is, taken as not needing to be argued and simply to be taken for granted. At least three reasons for the dominating and determining position of materialism in late modernity can be given.

The first is that materialism, which is sometimes called "physicalism" or "naturalism," refers to practical limits that are put on what can publicly be talked about and is open to general agreement. In a diverse culture, both academic and general, it is necessary to establish limits on any discursive situation, to recognize what is in and what is out of bounds, and how the potential of the discursive situation can be furthered. While limits vary according to the kind of discursive situation that is operative, the limits that are generally assumed are materialist. To the degree that there is a shared culture, either academic or general, it can be identified as materialist. It determines what can profitably be talked about, what everyone thinks of as real, dependable, and shared, namely, what is or can be traced to entities and events or to matter and energy. When other interests are shared, such as feelings, opinions, goals, or beliefs, a noticeable exchange occurs, namely, from what is generally assumed to be shared to what is allowed by more personal or in other ways more limited situations.

While a common ground for discursive situations is of general and everyday cultural value, it is especially of value for academic and scholarly interactions and pursuits. It provides the methods, norms, and terms by which agreement and at least a degree of certainty can be reached. The operative assumption is that final authority should be given to entities and events as much as possible stripped of interpretations and evaluations. This role of materialism and the authority of facts within academic culture need not be made operative before the discursive situation occurs; they are assumed not only in any academic situation but also supported by their roles in the wider culture.

It is important to note that the social, cultural, and academic roles and authority granted to and created by practical materialism are widely seen not only as a method or convention for establishing a way of actualizing the positive potentials of discursive situations but also as descriptive of how we and other people actually are in and relate to the world. Practical materialism not only provides common grounds for diverse interests and for ways of securing a degree of discursive firmness; it is also an assumption that materialism can adequately account for our world and our relations within and to it. However important personal convictions or interests may be, persons can generally be counted on to suspend them under the pressure of a culturally shared sense of the basic standing and shared role of material. It is fair to say that this assumption has a built-in hierarchy. It finds its most authoritative and influential place in scientific laboratories; it extends more broadly into academic culture; it forms the basis for legal, political, business, and other circles of interest; and it moves finally into discourses of more casual kinds. So widespread and ingrained are assumptions and practices determined by materialism that persons are often and to some significant degree taken to be materially identifiable. When we encounter other people, we tend to understand them first of all in materialist terms, most obviously their need, desire, and potential to survive and prosper. Anything else that we take as part of our worlds, other kinds of relations, interpretations, and values, if they cannot be related to the need for people physically or materially to establish and secure themselves, become secondary and more individuating than shareable.

While these assumptions, conditions, and priorities need not, indeed cannot, be wholly challenged, it should be made clear that they are themselves not necessarily natural but cultural. Western culture was not always so materialistically understood. Persons were, and in some contexts continue to be, primarily understood, to use shorthand terms, by their values and beliefs. It is not as though cultures, including Western modernity, first gather materially based knowledge and then apply to it values and beliefs. Values and beliefs form and continue for many to affect inquiry and the need for what is shareable and certain. People forget that the current authority and basic role of materialism is a cultural convention and not descriptive of how we actually are in and relate to our world. This cultural and academic convention is a way of doing things and has itself taken on a factual or natural standing and role. When it does, the beliefs and values that people have are assigned a secondary, personal, and optional standing because beliefs and values lack shared acceptance. Finally, when this cultural convention or assumption takes on the status of reality and fact, materialism comes no longer to be taken as something that needs to be argued but as simply and obviously the case.

It should first of all be seen that at both the macro and micro levels, matter and energy are far from simply and obviously there. While matter and energy for physicists provide, thanks primarily to mathematics, a degree of certainty and methodological consistency, matter and energy, rather than providing a firm and clear base, are always also bringing up new questions, uncertainties, and even mysteries. It becomes clear that it is not only "facts" that form the basis of agreement but also, perhaps even more, the need for agreement as to when and why something deserves to be named and treated as a fact. What we take to be a fact can always be further interrogated or dissected. Facts, then, are not simply obvious and self-warranting. What determines a fact depends also on cultural agreement as to what can be taken as factual, shareable, and certain. Entities and events become facts in part when cultural assumptions determine that they are factual enough.

I do not think that these questions concerning the use of materialism to set the terms of discourse in academic and wider culture are sufficient to undermine their standing or to reject abiding by their limits. The usefulness of this way of doing things is too manifest to oppose. But I also do not think that its standing should be descriptive of the way we actually are or should be in the world. Its limited, practical, and conventional standing and role should be more often pointed out and made recognizable, and the importance of inquiry concerning the ends and means that govern actions and of evaluations concerning their relations to human well-being should have a prominence and urgency equal to that determined by materialist norms.

A second way in which I have been using the term materialism is in reference to the primary and determining environments that modernity has produced. Something not unique but uniquely important occurs in Western culture near the beginning of the nineteenth century and with increasing visibility during the ensuing Victorian period. While the process has deep and various roots, its cumulative effects exert a powerful and consequential cultural force. I have referred to it by its manifestations in industrialization, urbanization, mobility, and means of communication. Perhaps the first of these is the most important. The technological developments that produced more massive means of production resulted both in the concentration of people, especially workers, in the locations of production, causing increasing numbers of people to live in larger cities, and in the development of new forms of mobility and communication that would make movement, including access to the materials needed for production and to the markets needed for distributing products, increasingly possible. What occurred, then, was the development of a culture in which the lives of people became increasingly incorporated into and determined by humanly constructed and operated environments and the kinds of human interrelationships created and required by them.

Crucial to the rise and spread of this culture is the endorsing assumption that all of this represents advancement and progress and that it indicates not merely some parts or practices of the culture but is descriptive of the culture in its basis and/or entirety. While the negative and even destructive side of this advancing culture at times becomes noticeable, such as the degradation and entrapment of people by urban spaces and the environmental damage caused by developments characteristic of modernity, not to speak of modern warfare as an inevitable aspect of modern culture, it carries with it a sense of its own entitlement due mainly to its reputation of being natural and inevitable. Resistances and alternatives to it break out, but such opposition has only to be weathered so that the determining power of material advancement and its assumed benefits can continue unimpeded.

CONCLUSION

Today, we live in a culture that is understood and actualized materially. More than half of the world's population lives in large cities, and more efficient forms of communication and transportation are in the process of sponsoring a new globalization. These changes cannot be resisted; we are carried along and conditioned by them. True, we preserve and visit natural areas; we value personal interests and self-determination; and we admire people who act in ways that reveal regard for the well-being of others. But these and other such matters have the standing and role of exceptions to the overriding presence and influence of environments that are material and are constructed and driven by the desire for advancement, increased power, and security. Those who exhibit actions and attitudes that differ from those environments tend to be seen as exceptions, while those who are not sufficiently empowered to participate and prosper in a culture so constructed are marginalized, oppressed, or exploited by it, devalued, or, at best, pitied.

As I pointed out at the beginning of this guide, various cultural counter-movements and emphases have arisen and continue to be heard, an especially broad and influential form of them related to Romanticism and its continuing manifestations and consequences. I have suggested that religious studies gained cultural importance by drawing attention to the human matters that the expanding and otherwise unimpeded materialist culture lacked or failed to provide. In my opinion, whatever lessens and questions the impact of a materialist culture on us should be regarded as of possible value, and studying religion is one of them. If nothing else, aspects of Romanticism and the study of religion culturally support one another by pointing out that materialist accounts of the human world and of the relations of people in and to it are partial at best and potentially reductive and repressive at worst.

In addition to these two uses of the term materialism, that is, as referring to a way of operating in a diverse culture and to the kind of environments in which the majority of people live, there is a third form or use of the term, namely, theoretical. This is the conscious assumption or view that anything that exists or occurs can be causally traced to or adequately explained in material terms, that is, in terms of matter and energy. While this theory has a tradition and supports of its own, it has its primary base in the natural sciences because it is implied by the scientific method. As already stated, that method has two primary components. The first is to strip whatever is under investigation as much as possible of previously held interpretations and evaluations in order to see what is under investigation reliably, to view it, in a word, objectively. The second component of the scientific method is to reduce what is under investigation as much as possible to its most elementary constituents. The point I have tried to lodge is that this method has spread from its particular arena and occasions to its acceptance in academic culture more widely and to a way of viewing human life more generally. Human beings take one another as inhabiting a world materially constituted and addressing it primarily as separable from whatever evaluations or goals it may carry with it or that have been projected on it.

Theoretical materialism as a consciously formed view of everything has its cultural standing not so much on the basis of the arguments made in its support as by the prestige of modern science. Indeed, materialism is less a consciously formed and defended theory and more a governing and pervasive assumption or force, in a word, an ideology. I at times find people surprised, if not offended, when I suggest that the point of view they reveal in what they say is essentially materialist. They even think I am calling them Marxist. While there are deliberate spokespersons for theoretical materialism, for the most part, it is implied by the positions people generally and unintentionally take. This means that theoretical materialism has had, in the arena of theory, an easy time of it. It need not be defended as an adequate account of our world, our selves, and our relations within and to our world; it is simply already there, assumed as a natural, realistic, or up-to-date way of thinking and acting. Alternative positions are relegated to the margins or to the past and are at best tolerated as isolated or personal whimsies or intrusions.

I tend to think, given the culture in which we find ourselves, that it is not possible successfully to contend against theoretical materialism, either in its popular or in its sophisticated form. One reason for this is that alternative positions to it have been assigned to the margins of discourse, including academic culture. The playing field is constructed by and for materialist assumptions, and alternative views are put in the position of having to argue that they should be allowed to play on that field. Alternatives are put in the negative position of being obstacles, oddities, or diversions. The most that can be done is to argue that theoretical materialism offers an inadequate view of who we are, of the world in which we find ourselves, and of our relations to and within it. Two ways to advance this argument come immediately to mind.

The first is to remind ourselves that any view we have of our world and our position in it is a product of our awareness, thinking, and believing. Indeed, what is most obvious, real, and natural to us is that we think, feel, perceive, respond, create, and decide. The material, especially when taken as free from our thinking about it, is, compared to our general dispositions and behaviors, somewhat odd and alien. Romanticism, generally considered, has, despite its excesses and limitations, done a great service by insisting on the enduring importance and even primacy of things we associate with our being persons. What makes us persons is primary to us both in status and meaning, and matter and energy are, relative to being a person or having an identity, secondary.

It is not surprising that various kinds of philosophical idealism are interwoven with forms of Romanticism. I think, indeed, that such support is needed. However, without simply discrediting any extant forms of philosophical or theoretical idealism, I think it is fair to say that the nonmaterial has its place more effectively in human experiences than in argument. I have in mind such matters of awareness as the reliability of mathematics and intuition for physicists and the non-accountability of so many things that we admire, such as creative artistry and the edifying effects on us that the lives of morally admirable people can have. Such things—and many others, some more widely encountered and more deeply important—give people not only awareness of what can be thought of as spiritual, edifying, or ideal but also a desire for and a high evaluation of them. It is my guess that more people are incipient or occasional idealists than intentional and consistent materialists.

While artistic and other noticeable creative human acts testify to the continuing role and importance of the spiritual, ideal, and edifying potentials in persons and the culture, they are, almost by definition, isolated and, by being so, vulnerable to materialist interests, especially financial. Whatever supports what is more comprehensive and indelible in human history and current life should be taken seriously, and that something, it seems to me, is religious. The study of religion directs attention to and can create understanding and even appreciation for matters of great, even primary, importance to us that are neglected or cannot be accounted for by the materialism that, in ways I have indicated, conditions Western culture.

The study of religion can play the role in academic culture of calling to attention human needs and potentials that the current culture neglects or cannot provide only if it takes religion as at least a serious cultural interest and formulates methods for understanding and even appreciating it. It may be personally flattering for a scholar in religious studies to occupy a position deemed superior to the religious people studied because the beliefs and practices of those studied are considered to be outgrown or marginalized. However, what needs to be done is to take the religion of religious people not lightly, as a curiosity, anomaly, or vestige, but as, among other things, a calling to attention and offering response to important but culturally neglected factors in what makes us human.

In order to do this, the study of religion, while it can derive much from methods and findings from other studies in the humanities and social sciences, cannot adopt the implicit materialism that will likely be assumed by them. Another way of saying this is that the study of religion cannot take as its method or goal an understanding of what religion is or what religious people are like that is contrary to or dismissive of what religious people believe, experience, and practice. A nonreligious or materialist approach to the study of religion is as misplaced or inadequate as is a non-aesthetic approach to art or a non-mathematical approach to physics. Whether for religious or nonreligious reasons, the investigator cannot assume to know what actually is the case or to have adequate, especially nonreligious, explanations for or alternatives to what is being studied.

II

We turn, now, in the other direction, namely, away from the materialistically affected academic culture to confessional or religiously specific positions and institutions regarding the study of religion. The principal question raised by confessional bases or identities for a department of religious studies is that a religious basis for study is taken, in both nonreligiously identified academic and also general culture, not to be part of public or shared life. This separation is not simply the effect of nonreligious people opposing the imposition of religious interests on their own or on public life, although that is certainly operative. The principal reason is that religious people will also tend, especially if their form of religion is prophetic or priestly, to locate themselves or their religion in a realm separate from, if not contrary or superior to, the general or shared culture or to interpret the culture in ways conforming to their own religiously governed beliefs and norms. While in other countries the separation of religious and nonreligious forms of educational and research interests tends to be identifiable institutionally, the United States, while also marked by institutional distinctions, has a culture in which religious interests continue to be noticeably active.

One matter to be considered is that when we refer to a person or group as religious, we will likely have in mind priestly and/or prophetic religious elements. We will likely have in mind beliefs or behaviors that to a detectable degree differ from those characteristic of nonreligious persons or groups, such as praying, participating faithfully in religious institutional life, or accounting for things and events in religiously identifiable ways. Personal and group religious identities, consequently, carry the effect of being exceptional. This effect is not only projected by others; it is also likely to be intended by the person's religious actions and discourse. It is not a surprise, therefore, that being different and being religious are easily combined. And difference by means of religion will, at least to some noticeable degree, cash out as qualitative, particularly of being not only different but also superior. This quality is not only personal but is also generated by group identity.

There are several forms that religious group separation and superiority are manifested in, although not confined to, contemporary America. One of them is quite dispersed, although it also takes institutional forms. Its most noticeable manifestation is fundamentalism and, in the case of Protestant Christianity, evangelicalism. While these two forms are distinguishable from one another, they are historically and culturally related. One sign of their continuing kinship is that they tend to share a largely negative view of the culture and to think of it as needing to be avoided, altered, or replaced. This means that religious identity stands apart from the shared and contrary to the general culture in a realm secured by personal, group, or institutional religious principles. As I pointed out earlier, it is not surprising that on academic campuses, especially on those that have no institutional religious identities, student groups are formed around religious dynamics of this kind and have been and continue to be successful. They address a need that the academic culture creates by its secular and materialist methods, assumptions, or ideology. They also provide social and personal interactions that are welcomed alternatives to competitive academic dynamics and reduced forms of socializing in a nonreligiously informed student culture. It can be said that religious studies in academic culture should not stand in total separation from such interests because religious studies also needs to be warranted by the academic value of religious understandings of human needs, potentials, and well-being.

Religious separatism takes another form, namely, institutional. This is clear when religious institutions restrict participation in their rites to those who qualify to be numbered among their members. This form of separation is not confined to American culture or to Christianity. For religious groups and institutions, some degree of distinction, at times a high degree, is made between those who are on the inside and those who are not.

Religious separatism also takes a third, more academic form, based on current theories of differing and opposing discursive situations and traditions. Like fundamentalism and evangelicalism, these forms of exceptionalism place people in currents or traditions of meaning detached from, even contrary to, those created by other currents, including modern culture. As I mentioned earlier, two visible and influential sources of this form of religious separatism are so-called radical or neo-orthodoxy and religious traditionalism. A very interesting set of connections is presently created, then, by the overlapping or conjoining of otherwise separate forms of religious separateness and identity, traditionalism, evangelicalism or fundamentalism, and ecclesiastical or institutional separatism.

Religious separation finds support in academic settings from the general turn of social sciences, especially anthropology, in the latter half of the twentieth century, from Enlightenment or universal understandings of human life and cultures to more particularized understandings, a change that found support in various forms of discourse analysis and tradition-based theories of cultural continuity and coherence. These academic changes support the assumption that religious identity, like cultural identity, is primarily centripetal and separable from, if not in opposition to, others.

Despite their differences, it should be understood that the basis of these forms of separatism is also religious. It rests on the dominance of the "x" and/or "y" factor and a prophetic and/or priestly form of religion. In their more extreme formations, these options lessen or repress the "z" factor of a more fully actualized religious system, that is, the role of concern for human needs, potentials, and well-being. They are partial and exclusionary because they are defined by prophetic and priestly components at the expense of the sapiential component of religion. While understanding and appreciation of the reasons for various forms of religious separatism in both academic and in wider cultures, a religious studies department, while it should be related to sites where such religious interests are defining, must also distinguish itself from them. It must both understand them and exert pressure on them concerning the need for due attention to sapiential religious factors, especially human needs, potentials, and well-being, including those shared by religiously differing people and those who are not religiously identifiable.

III

The question that remains is how a department of religious studies can establish and maintain a position that distinguishes it from the Scylla of academic materialism and the Charybdis of religious, confessional, or ecclesiastical separatism while also maintaining appreciation, understanding, and relations with both. In a word, what sources are available to ground a department so conceived and situated? It has been my goal throughout to give an answer to this question. I shall summarize it by rehearsing what I take to be the two major supports for an answer.

The first, as I have already suggested, is cultural, and one cultural current in which it appears and becomes dominant is in Western modernity generally and in Romanticism particularly. One may be surprised that the choice here is not the Enlightenment, since it forms a tradition of high intellectual standards that often also took religion, although within limits, positively into account. At the risk of seeming hasty, I see the Enlightenment, while in important and continuing ways representative of the involvement of religious and cultural/intellectual interests with one another, as primarily constrictive. "Limits" is not only a recurring but also a characteristic term for this cultural climate or tradition, and rational limits on religious discourses, like the imposition of political and social restraints, effectively cordons off or sets the terms of what is and what is not admissible. The effects of this positioning of religion within limits continue to be felt. Religion continues to be taken as tolerable if it is confined, but such consignment serves more to marginalize than to legitimize it. Romanticism was, along with much else, a breaking out of these and other limits. More importantly, it was a cultural movement that sought, as I have tried to point out, to retrieve, grant access to, and expand resources that were deemed lacking or marginalized in an increasingly materialist culture and relevant to human well-being. Romanticism was, consequently, supportive of interest in the study of religion. Its legacy carries within it recurring spiritual or non-material emphases and attention to important aspects of human life to which materialist accounts cannot do justice.

Without rehearsing what already has been said, Romanticism to some degree has continuing effects on modern culture that support in various ways the study of religion, the meaningful role of religion in human life, and the need, in giving an account of human life, to include religious needs, interests, and constructions. It is this intellectual and cultural tradition, selectively treated and appropriately revised, to which a department of religious studies should do justice. In doing so, it should, while also selective and remolding, emphasize the cultural lacks and faults to which Romanticism forms a response and that continue, and these lacks and faults should be turned toward religion as a major resource by which they and their debilitating personal and cultural consequences can be redressed.

The second and broader source upon which departments of religious studies so conceived can draw are sapiential religious traditions or the sapiential aspects of more complex traditions. When describing the three forms that religions can and largely do take, I described the sapiential form of Western Christianity as having its primary textual and religious basis in biblical wisdom literature. The wisdom literature is marked by attention to the natural world, by an understanding of differing cultures, by the need to deal positively with culturally and religiously differing people, and by identifying and giving reasons for admiring and emulating wise, creative, and morally admirable persons and aspects of culture. Prophetic and priestly elements can and do enter the wisdom texts, but the primary emphasis is on the complexity, even wonder, of the natural world, on the rich diversity of human societies and cultures and their relations to one another, and on the values and goals that make human beings better, particularly in moral and spiritual ways, than they are.

A religious studies department should emphasize the sapiential forms that appear in religious traditions and make these religious forms more explicit. This suggestion is not arbitrary. In my view, modernity is grounded in, comprehended by, and indebted to sapiential religious systems that, while appearing in various ways throughout the tradition, came to cultural prominence in early modernity and challenged the primarily priestly forms of medieval Christianity and the primarily prophetic forms of Protestantism.

Romanticism and sapiential religion overlap in that both, in differing ways and with differing effects, combine religious and cultural interests. This does not mean that faculty in departments of religious studies ought to self-identify as either Romantic or religiously sapiential. Rather, this is how they should understand where historically, culturally, and academically they most immediately stand and how they can formulate more clearly and substantially their academic place and role. The texts, methods, and interests pursued should be affected by an appreciation of the relations of religion and modernity that are provided by conjoining these two continuing but undervalued traditions, namely Romanticism and sapiential religious forms. These two traditions are not minor moments in the formation of Western modernity, and they have not been outgrown. They are major resources that continue to be needed as both critical of the culture and contributory to it.

Those in departments of religious studies are enabled to identify themselves by pointing to sapiential forms of their own religious traditions or of those they study and by affirming them as not sporadic or secondary but as constant, basic, and complex. In turn, they can respond to more prophetic and priestly advocates of religion by pointing out that sapiential forms of religion are not watered-down versions of other religious forms but have their own integrity, sources, and consequences. On the other hand, members of a department of religious studies can turn to their colleagues in other departments and, in ways they will recognize, point out how religion is embedded in, supportive of, and critical relative to human culture and that modernity also carries this form of religion or traces of it as an enabling, deepening, and challenging participant that can and deserves to be taken more fully into account.

While I place attention to the sapiential element in religions between the recognizable contraries of a religious and a nonreligious basis for the study of religion, I think a more critical point should be made concerning that position. It is, as I think I have already made clear, that academic culture has increasingly turned toward material accounts of human life and culture. To put the matter sharply, I do not think that the kinds of religious scholarship described in the first part of this book, particularly its view of religion as deeply involved in human life and culture, can be expected in work governed by the present methods and interests in the social sciences and humanities. This raises the question as to whether or not academic culture has the means to put forward scholarship that is based on norms and values that are shared and supported. This leads me to propose that departments of religious studies should be open to revivals of interest in the matters that are parts of a more complete understanding of religion, namely, matters that I labeled as prophetic and priestly. Can the morals and values traditionally carried by academic culture be supported by religion governed solely by human interests and concern for them? This question opens up the need and possibility of a more involved participation by religious studies in matters of a priestly and prophetic kind. The current materialist direction of academic culture warrants and even requires an interest in and use of arguments in support of the contention that materialism is not a sufficient resource for understanding human life and culture. There need not only be a recognition of its inadequacy for understanding and advancing human life and culture but also a need to retrieve or reconstitute what it might mean to call prophetically for a more serious and shared interest in what transcends human understanding and control and for a priestly call as to how and why what transcends human understanding and control can be made available as altering or redirecting persons and their cultures.

As I said earlier, a position that is taken between clear and contrary alternatives is usually less clear and firm than the two sides to which it retains relations and also differs from them. The two positions I have opposed and to which I offer a mediating alternative are not only more clearly but also more firmly established. I do not expect that this guide has given adequate clarification and defense to convince those on either side, but it is hoped that it will provide a basis and occasion to examine and reevaluate the situation as it presently exists.

INDEX

Abrams, M. H. 10
Adams, Henry 8
Altman, Irwin 85n2
American Academy of Religion xix
Aristotle 9

Bachofen, J. J. 16–18, 27, 107
Bacon, Francis 4, 6
Barbeau, Jeffrey 10n1
Barth, Karl 123, 136, 137
beliefs, nonreligious 54, 66, 75, 76, 113, 132
Bellah, Robert 49–52, 110
biblical wisdom literature 94–95, 131
Buddhism xiv, xviii, 139–40
Burgess, Jacquelin 85n2

Calvinism vi, 4, 134, 136
Cambridge University 22
Campbell, Joseph 25
Catholic Christianity xiii, 20, 24, 43, 44, 92–93
charismatic leaders 46
civil religion 50–51
Constantine 9
cultural criticism 82–83

Darwin, Charles 37, 57
de Tocqueville, Alexis 37
death 36, 60
Duke University vii–viii
Durkheim, Emile 43–45, 47, 51, 109–10

Eliade, Mircea 69–71, 111
Enlightenment 152
environment, lack of concern for 33

evangelicalism 151
evolutionary theory 36, 39, 49, 60

Feuerbach, Ludwig 137
Frazer, James G 22–25, 36, 108
Freud, Sigmund xvi, 26, 62–66, 82, 111
Frye, Northrop 25

Geertz, Clifford 72–74, 112
Gold, John R. 85n2

Harvard University 39, 49
Herberg, Will xii–xiii
Hesse, Hermann 140
hetaerism 17
Hinduism xiv, xix, 19, 133
historical studies xv

Idealism 22
identity, personal and group 37, 43, 45, 47, 53–56, 133
imperialism 5
Islam xviii, xix, 9, 49, 72

James, William 27, 39–42, 47, 109
Judaism xiii, 43, 44, 70, 129
Jung, Carl Gustav 26–27, 69, 108

Kant, Immanuel 20, 133, 135
Kerouac, Jack 140
Kuyper, Abraham vi

liminality 28–30
linguistics 21, 73
Locke, John 138
Low, Sethham 85n2

magic 67, 68, 75, 111
Malinowski, Bronislaw 66–69, 75, 111

Marx, Karl xvi, 62, 63, 82, 122, 123, 148
masculinity 27, 33
materialism vi, xvi, 5, 11, 58, 61, 65, 80, 81, 101, 106, 114, 124, 127, 133, 140, 142, 146–49
matriarchy 16–18, 26
Merton, Thomas 140
myth 18, 22, 26, 27, 37, 50, 69, 70

nationalism 5
native American 32
nature, as second scripture 4–5

ontology 38, 39, 41, 43, 109
Otto, Rudolf 27, 133–37
Oxford University 19, 59, 72

patriarchy 17–18
personal identity 53–54
phenomenology 69
Plato 9
pragmatism 39
priestly religion 90–92, 109–10
Princeton University vi–vii, 72
profane, the 44, 68, 71, 109, 111
prophetic religion 91–92, 107–9
Protestant Christianity xiii, xv, xvii, 4, 20, 21, 43, 45, 50, 84, 120, 126, 135, 151

Rational Choice Theory 51
Reardon, Bernard 10n1
Reformation, the 92–93, 130
ritual 28–30, 43, 44, 50, 67, 70, 108–9, 112

Romanticism 7–8, 10, 15, 20, 22, 25, 27, 30, 40, 55, 58, 83, 101, 113–14, 127, 135, 147, 149, 153
Royce, Josiah 39

sacred, the 44, 70, 71, 109
Schleiermacher, Friedrich 40, 127, 135
scientific method 6, 66, 81
slavery 32–33
Smith, Jonathan Z. 84–85, 102
Society of Biblical Literature xix
Spencer, Herbert 35–40, 45, 109
spirituality 54–55, 140
sublimity 40
Suzuki, D. T. 140

temporality, human 55–56, 71, 76, 111
textuality 19
Thirty Years' War 3
totem 44, 67, 69, 109
Turner, Victor 28–30, 108–9
Tylor, Edward B. 59–62, 65, 110–11

University of Chicago vi
urbanization 6, 10, 15

van der Leeuw, Gerardus 69
van Gennep, Arnold 28

Weber, Max 46–49, 72, 90
Wittgenstein, Ludwig 72
World Wars I and II xi–xii, xvi, 84, 100, 102, 120, 123, 136, 139

Milton Keynes UK
Ingram Content Group UK Ltd.
UKHW012326131223
434319UK00003B/40